D1802387

# LIVING IN GOD'S GRACE

*ALLEN J. FOSS*

*APOSTLES' CREED
SACRAMENTS*

FAITH & FELLOWSHIP PRESS
704 W. Vernon Avenue - Box 655
Fergus Falls, MN 56537-0655

**All rights reserved. No part of this book may be reproduced or transmitted in any form or by any means, electronic or mechanical, including photocopying, recording, or by any information storage and retrieval system, without permission in writing from the publisher.**

Scripture text, unless otherwise indicated, is taken from the *Holy Bible, New International Version,* Copyright 1973, 1978 by the International Bible Society, used by permission of Zondervan Bible Publishers.

**Copyright © 1988, Faith and Fellowship Press**
**704 West Vernon Avenue - Box 655**
**Fergus Falls, Minnesota 56537-0655**
**ISBN# 0-943167-06-X**

# Preface

The Bible and the *Explanation of Luther's Small Catechism,* edited by Warren Olsen and David Rinden (Fergus Falls, Minnesota: Faith and Fellowship Press, 1988) are the texts for this study of thirty lessons. *Living in God's Grace* was written for use in confirmation classes but may be used by anyone wishing to understand the teachings of the Christian church.

The lessons consist of an introduction to the creeds, The Apostles' Creed, and the Sacraments. Each lesson has a reading assignment in the Bible, a reading and memorization assignment in *Explanation of Luther's Small Catechism,* and an explanation of the lesson and a worksheet.

There are three unit tests for this series of lessons. If this book is used in a confirmation class, the class teacher may wish to remove these tests before the books are distributed to the students. Each correct answer on the worksheet is worth three percentage points, and each correct answer on the unit tests is worth one percentage point for the true or false questions and two percentage points for the remaining questions.

Pastor Allen Foss, the author of this book, is pastor of Hope Lutheran Brethren Church, Everett, Washington. He has also served congregations in Aitkin, Minnesota; Bottineau, North Dakota; Ottawa, Illinois; and East Hartland, Connecticut. He has served as President of the Eastern District of the Church of the Lutheran Brethren and as a board member of the Lutheran Brethren Synod's Executive Board and Board of Home Missions. Pastor Foss was graduated from the Lutheran Brethren Seminary, Fergus Falls, Minnesota, in 1963, and from Concordia College, Moorhead, Minnesota, in 1959. Pastor Foss was a science teacher at the public school in New Rockford, North Dakota, prior to entering the Christian ministry. Pastor Foss and his wife, Goldie, are the parents of three children, Mark, Joel and Deborah. He is a native of Maddock, North Dakota.

Thanks is given to Pastor Foss for writing this book. Thanks is also given to Warren Olsen, Marjorie Rueckert and Pastors Eugene Boe, Dale Hanson and Everald H. Strom who read the manuscript and offered many suggestions.

This book is published with the prayer that all who read and study it will desire to live in God's grace.

David Rinden, Editor

**First Edition — 1988**

**Revised Edition — 1990**

Cover Design by Vera Carlson
Illustrations by Lynn Sunwall

# Table of Contents

*Continued on next page*

## Unit III - The Sacraments

# Introduction

*Do your best to present yourself to God as one approved, a workman who does not need to be ashamed and who correctly handles the word of truth. II Timothy 3:14-15*

The primary purpose of these lessons is to introduce the reader to the need of personal salvation and its provision in Jesus Christ. These lessons deal with the Apostles' Creed and its meaning, the Sacrament of Baptism and its meaning, and the Sacrament of the Lord's Supper and its meaning.

## The Goal of This Instruction

The main purpose of studying God's Word is to know Jesus Christ as Savior and to grow in the Christian life. Likewise, the purpose or the goal of these lessons is that you might come to know the saving grace of God in Christ. These lessons are also written that you might receive the sustaining grace of God which is able to equip you and strengthen you for effective Christian service. This is what the Apostle Paul said in II Timothy 2:15: "Do your best, work hard and be a diligent student of the Word, that you might be prepared and equipped for every good work." You are dependent upon the Holy Spirit and prayer to understand and handle the word of truth correctly. Therefore, pray daily that the Lord will help you to understand His Word and apply it to your life.

## The Textbooks for This Instruction

We will use three main textbooks. The first and primary textbook is the Bible. Therefore, it is necessary for you to have a Bible in which you may mark certain passages. Your study and memory work will be from the *New International Version (NIV)* of the Bible. Therefore, it is recommended that you use this version during this course of study. The Bible is the main textbook because it is the final source of authority when it comes to Christian faith and practice.

**Explanation of
Luther's Small Catechism**

The second textbook will be *Explanation of Luther's Small Catechism*. This book contains *The Small Catechism* written by Martin Luther. When he discovered that many people were either confused about spiritual truth or were not receiving it at all, he wrote this doctrinal summary of the Bible in 1529. A study of the Catechism is valuable and important for the following reasons:

1. The contents of the Catechism are taken from the Scriptures. The main teachings of the Bible are arranged in a brief system which is easy to understand.

2. The Catechism is one of the main works of the Reformation, and it continues to be a chief means of spreading and establishing the Christian faith.

3. The Catechism is one of the so-called *Symbols* of the Lutheran Church. That is, it is one of the confessions of the Christian faith.

4. It was through the witness of Martin Luther for Jesus Christ that the Lutheran Church came into being.

5. It is loved by those who become acquainted with its contents and who desire to know the revealed truth of God.

The third textbook will be this book, including the worksheets, which you are to complete each week. You will be expected to study these pages carefully as you prepare each lesson.

## Your Pastor's Concern

If you are using this book as a text for confirmation instruction, you should know that your pastor will always seek to be helpful to you. Ask him for further explanation if there is anything you do not understand in this book. Your pastor is your friend and your spiritual shepherd. He is anxious to help you in any way that he is able. He will keep secret anything you tell him in confidence.

# Confirmation Instruction Requirements

### Attendance

1. Class attendance is a part of confirmation instruction. Regular attendance is required. You are responsible for all assignments missed while absent from class. You may receive the assignment either by calling your pastor or one of your classmates.

2. Sunday morning worship services are a part of confirmation instruction. Regular attendance is expected of each student.

3. Sunday school Bible classes are a part of confirmation instruction. Regular attendance is expected of each student.

### Written Work

1. All worksheets are due at the beginning of each class period. The lesson sheets will be corrected and returned to you. They should be kept and used for reviewing your lessons in preparation for the test at the end of each unit of study.

2. Other written assignments may be given as homework. You will be responsible for completing this work regularly and on time.

3. Written quizzes may be given at the beginning of each class period on the material assigned for the day. A written test will be given at the end of each unit of study.

4. You will be required to hand in the notes from sermons. These notes are to include:
    1. Your name;
    2. Date;
    3. Bible text;
    4. Sermon title;
    5. Sermon notes should consist of the main points of the sermon, numbered I, II, III, etc., and a sentence or two under each point.

## Memory Work

1. Questions and Bible verses from the *Explanation of Luther's Small Catechism* will be assigned for memorization. Your pastor may assign any or all of these questions and verses. You are to be prepared not only to quote them from memory but also to write them out correctly.

2. At the end of the year you will be given a group of questions and verses to review and know perfectly. Your pastor will ask you to recite some of these questions and verses at the public catechization.

3. Other assignments may be given from time to time.

# Introduction to the Creeds

*Assignment*

Read Acts 1. Study questions 120-126 in the *Explanation of Luther's Small Catechism.* Read this lesson, complete the worksheet and be prepared for a quiz.

*I am not ashamed, because I know whom I have believed, and am convinced that he is able to guard what I have entrusted to him for that day. II Timothy 1:12b*

## Christian Knowledge

As Christians, we should grow in our knowledge of the content of the Christian faith. While saving faith is personal trust in Jesus, we should desire to know more about this One who has forgiven us our sin. As we grow in knowledge of our God and Savior, we should be able to express this knowledge in our own words. Many centuries ago those who came to faith in Jesus Christ made up certain statements to express what they personally believed about God. These expressions of faith are called *creeds.*

# What Is a Creed?

A creed is a statement of what a person believes. The word *creed* comes from the Latin word *credo,* which means, *I believe.* A creed, therefore, is a statement of belief, or a confession of faith. Since the highest authority is the Bible, the Bible alone is the final rule of faith and life. The teaching in the creeds comes from the Bible.

All people have a particular belief. It may be that some believe there is no God. If this is what they believe, this becomes their creed, their belief. Christians believe in the God who has revealed Himself to them in the Bible. This, then, becomes the Christian's creed or belief.

# Kinds of Creeds

There are two kinds of Christian creeds. These two kinds of creeds are the *universal* creeds and the *particular* creeds. These creeds are also called *confessions of faith.* The universal creeds, accepted by the entire Christian Church, are:

1. The Apostles' Creed - Written as a statement of faith by the early church to refute and stand against the influ-ence of false teachings.

2. The Nicene Creed - Written in 325 A.D. at the Council of Nicea to declare the deity of Christ, that Christ is God, one with the Father and begotten of the Father from eternity.

3. The Athanasian Creed - Written in the 5th or 6th century. It says that if Christ is not God, He cannot be our Savior.

Two particular creeds, accepted by the Lutheran Church, are:

1. The Augsburg Confession - Written after the Reformation and presented to the Diet of Augsburg in 1530.

2. The Small Catechism - Written by Martin Luther in order that children might understand and become thoroughly grounded in the Scriptures.

Universal creeds are sometimes called *ecumenical creeds.* Almost all Protestant churches, together with the Roman Catholic Church, accept these three creeds as a true statement of the Christian faith.

There are false religions which do not accept these statements of belief. Therefore, we do not consider them to be members of the Christian faith. Some of these false religions are: The Jehovah's Witnesses, Christian Science and the Church of Jesus Christ of Latter Day Saints. Much of what they teach cannot be found in the Bible.

Particular creeds are the creeds which are accepted by a particular denomination or group. These are the distinctive statements of doctrine or beliefs of these groups. These particular creeds are often explanations of the universal creeds, or the teachings in the Bible.

## The Apostles' Creed

The best-known creed is the Apostles' Creed. It is a creed which is accepted by all Christians. This creed gives a brief statement of the content of the Christian faith.

Although it has the name Apostles' Creed, it was not written by the Apostles. It has this name because it is a brief summary of the teachings which the Apostles believed and taught. This creed has been used in the church through many centuries. We are not sure when it was originally written, but we believe it was revised and put into its present form about 750 A.D. It grew out of the original Trinitarian formula of baptism found in Matthew 28:19, "In the name of the Father and of the Son and of the Holy Spirit."

Just as the law is taught in the Ten Commandments, so the gospel is in the Apostles' Creed. We may say that the creed is a statement of the gospel which proclaims the works of God to us. It is not merely a set of theoretical phrases, for behind them stands the personal God, who actually gives salvation and permits us to know and experience His love.

In Luther's interpretation of the creed we see two points of view. One view is the objective reality of God who gives the gifts. The other view is of the gifts themselves, gifts given in order that we may come to faith in Him. The giver and the gift belong together, and neither can be understood without the other. What matters is a vital personal relationship between the giving God and us as His receiving people.

The creed does not say everything. It is intended merely to be a brief summary statement. Therefore, the creed is a good starting point for all study in the content of faith. It is the foundation for all Christian instruction, preaching and evangelism.

### The Three Articles

Sometimes the Apostles' Creed is called *The Three Articles*. It is called this because it contains three short paragraphs or statements. These statements tell of what Christians believe about God as He has revealed Himself to us as the Father, the Son and the Holy Spirit.

Article I- Tells us of God the Father and His work of creation.

Article II - Tells us of God the Son and His work of redemption.

Article III - Tells us of God the Holy Spirit and His work of sanctification.

## The Small Catechism

*The Small Catechism* is one of the particular creeds of the Lutheran Church. In this small book Martin Luther gives us short explanations of the teachings of the Christian faith. In it he also gives his explanation of the Apostles' Creed.

## The Triune God

The Apostles' Creed states belief in the Triune God. That is, it gives the activity of each of the three persons in the Godhead. Christians believe in the Triune God which is a trinity of persons. They believe that there is only one God, the creator and keeper of the universe and of His people. They believe that this one God has revealed Himself in the three persons of the Father, Son and Holy Spirit.

We cannot hope to understand this great truth. It is our privilege to believe it as taught in the Bible. We need to be aware of any religious teaching which claims to be Christian and yet denies the biblical doctrine of the Trinity. Among these are the Jehovah's Witness, Christian Science, Unitarian and Mormon religions.

Name _____

# Lesson One        Worksheet

*True or False.*

_____ 1. A Christian should desire continually to know more about Christ.

_____ 2. Many years ago Christians expressed what they believed in written statements.

_____ 3. We should be able to express our faith in our own words as we grow in the grace and knowledge of Christ.

_____ 4. The word *creed* comes from the Greek word *credo*, which means *I believe.*

_____ 5. A person's conscience is the final rule of faith and life.

_____ 6. Even those who worship the devil have a creed.

_____ 7. All people have a particular belief.

_____ 8. The Apostles' Creed contains twelve articles.

_____ 9. There are three kinds of Christian creeds.

_____ 10. The Universal Creeds are accepted by all Christian churches.

_____ 11. *The Small Catechism* is one of the particular creeds of the Lutheran Church.

_____ 12. The Athanasian Creed was written during the time of the Reformation.

_____ 13. The universal creeds are sometimes called Ecumenical Creeds.

_____ 14. Even though a church does not accept all three Universal Creeds, it may still be considered a member of the Christian faith.

_____ 15. Much of what Jehovah's Witnesses teach cannot be found in the Bible.

_____ 16. The Apostles' Creed was written by the Apostles.

_____ 17. The Apostles' Creed gives a brief statement of the Christian faith.

_____ 18. The best known creed of the Christian church is the Nicene Creed.

_____ 19. God gives us His gifts in order that we may come to faith in Him.

19

_____ 20. What matters most is a vital, personal relationship between the giving God and us as His receiving people.

_____ 21. The Apostles' Creed contains everything there is to know about the gospel.

_____ 22. The First Article tells us of God the Son and His work of redemption.

_____ 23. *The Small Catechism* was written by Dr. Martin Luther King.

_____ 24. God has revealed Himself to us in the three persons of the Father, Son and Holy Spirit.

_____ 25. We need to be aware of any religious group which claims to be Christian and yet denies the Biblical doctrine of the Trinity.

*Completion Questions.*

26. What is a creed?


27. Explain the difference between the universal creeds and the particular creeds.


28. What are the three universal creeds?
    a.
    b.
    c.


29. Why was *The Small Catechism* written?

30. What do the three articles teach us about God?

*Answer the following questions from your study of Acts 1.*

31. Where did Jesus say His disciples were to be His witnesses?

32. What happened to Jesus after He had said these things to the disciples?


33. Who was chosen to take Judas' place among the Apostles, and how was he chosen?

# The Triune God

*Assignment*

Read Acts 2. Memorize the First Article and its meaning. Study questions 127-132, including the First Article and its meaning, in the *Explanation of Luther's Small Catechism*. Read this lesson, complete the worksheet and be prepared for a quiz.

*Know that the Lord is God. It is he who made us, and we are his; we are his people, the sheep of his pasture. Enter his gates with thanksgiving and his courts with praise; give thanks to him and praise his name. Psalm 100:3-4*

## The First Article

I believe in God, the Father Almighty, maker of heaven and earth.

## I Believe

Each of the three articles of the Apostles' Creed begin with the words "I believe..." This is because, as stated in the previous lesson, a creed is a statement of faith. The

Apostles' Creed is a summary of what one believes as a Christian. Therefore, we do not say "we believe," but "I believe." It is the confession of a personal faith. "Believe in" does not mean merely that I believe that there is a God. It means that I trust in Him as my Father, rely wholly upon Him, and accept His Son as my Savior and Lord.

Faith is not superstition, nor is it being gullible. Neither is faith being persuaded to come to some intellectual conclusion. Faith is personal trust in God through Christ. The creed thus becomes the expression of a personal relationship to Him. If I do not know God as my Father, or Christ as my Savior, I cannot truthfully confess the Apostles' Creed.

We say "I believe," because no one can be saved by another person's faith. We must believe for ourselves. Just as we cannot eat or sleep for anyone else, neither can we believe for someone else. But you say, "My mother or my father is a Christian." I'm sorry, that will not save you. Salvation is a personal matter. You must say "I believe." Believe means "to trust," that is, "to take God at His word." Or we might say, believe means to *know* with the mind, to *assent* (to agree) with the lips, and to *trust* with the heart. For example: A drowning person knows the importance of a life belt. He assents to its power to save. He trusts it by grabbing hold of it.

I *know* the history of Christ's life and death. I *assent* to it as historically true. Saving faith goes one step farther. As a result of that history I *rely* upon it for my salvation. So the important thing about our faith is not merely to know and assent, but to trust.

True faith is depending on the word and promise of God. Depending on anything else is not faith but idolatry. Some say it does not matter so much *what* you believe, just *so* you believe. Could we not then say, "It does not matter so much what you eat, just so you eat?" What you believe molds and influences your whole life.

## God and His Work

The First Article of the Apostles' Creed speaks of God the Father and of His work of *creation.* In the previous lesson we stated that this God is a Triune God. By that we mean that God is one, but at the same time He has revealed Himself to us in the three distinct persons of the Father, Son and Holy Spirit. Although the word *Trinity* is not found in the Bible, it is clearly taught in the Bible and is fundamental to the plan of salvation.

The doctrine of the Trinity is not merely a theoretical one. Rather, it is very practical because our whole salvation depends upon it. It was revealed to us in God's plan of redemption. God the Father sent His Son into the world to save us, God the Son became man and redeemed us, and God the Holy Spirit applies the redemption of Christ to us. If there is no Trinity, then we are not saved, for then there is no Father to send His Son, no Son to atone for our sins, and no Holy Spirit to bring us to living faith in Christ our Savior.

In Genesis 1:26, we have an indication that God exists as more than one person. "Then God said, 'Let *us* make man in *our* image, in *our* likeness...'" Notice the pronouns which are used for God, such as: "us" and "our." In John 14:16-17, we find the Father, Son and Holy Spirit in close relationship to each other. In The Great Commission which Jesus gave and recorded in Matthew 28:18-20, we find that baptism is commanded in the name of the Father, and of the Son and of the Holy Spirit.

It must be emphasized that we do not believe in three gods. We believe in only one God. But at the same time, we believe that this one God is a Trinity, consisting of the Father, the Son, and the Holy Spirit. We admit that we cannot completely understand how this can all be, but the Bible presents this teaching and we believe it even if we cannot understand it all. If we could understand all that there is to know about God, then God would be no bigger than we are, and in fact, we would be like God. God would not be God if we could understand all about Him.

## What Is This Triune God Like?

People sometimes wonder what God is like. Some think of God as being something like an old, white-haired grandfather, who sits in a rocking chair all day. At the same time, they think this God would never really punish His grandchildren for being naughty. This is a false idea of God. If we are to learn what God is like, we must go to the Bible.

*God is a Spirit* - Jesus told us plainly that God is a Spirit (John 4:24). As a spirit, we are not able to see Him with our physical eyes. He does not have a physical body. The Bible often speaks of God as though He was a human being, having arms, hands, fingers and a face. This does not mean that God has the form of a human being. Instead, the Bible is using picture words which have meaning to us so that we might in a small way learn the true nature of the Spirit of God. The true God is not to be found in idols of wood, clay or stone. The true God is to be found through the Bible in which He has revealed Himself to us. As a Spirit, God is invisible to us.

*God is Living* - God is a living, intelligent, active being (Jeremiah 10:10). He is not to be thought of as an imaginary being existing in the minds of superstitious people. God is a living Spirit, very much alive and active. The Bible tells us that, "It is a dreadful thing to fall into the hands of the living God" (Hebrew 10:31). If we are unprepared to meet Him, then it will be a most fearful experience to fall into His hands at the judgment.

*God is Holy* - God Himself tells us that He is holy (Leviticus 11:44-45). To be "holy" means "to be set apart." In God there can be found no sin at all. At the same time the Bible tells us that this true and holy God demands of us that we be holy. It is dangerous to knowingly go against God's will as made known in the Commandments. God is holy and He demands holiness of life on the part of all people.

*God is All-Knowing* - God knows all things (I John 3:20). This may serve as a warning to us against sinning, for nothing can be hidden from Him (Hebrew 4:13). This may also serve as a comfort when we know that God knows the difficulties we may be having. I may be assured that He is faithful and will act on my behalf in due time.

*God is Faithful* - The true God of the Bible is also a faithful God to His own (I Corinthians 10:13). There may often come times when the child of God is tempted and tested, but the Bible assures us that God is faithful to provide the needed escape and endurance.

*God is Love* - As a God of love, we may be assured that He loves us (John 3:16). This God who is made known to us in the Bible is a wonderful God. He is a God of whom we must not be afraid if we desire to know Him.

He is a Spirit who is good and full of love and desires to give good gifts to His own.

*God is Good* - The Bible tells us that God is good (Psalm 118:1). This is an important truth to learn. It means that we need not be afraid to come to Him. It also means that there is no fault or defect in Him. All things that He does are good and meant to be good for us (Romans 8:28).

*Other Descriptions of God* - There are many other attributes of God which are given in the Bible. He is unchangeable (Psalm 102:26-27). He is everywhere present, not limited by space (I Kings 8:27), yet He is not far from any one of us, because in Him we live and move and have our being. God is also eternal (Psalm 90:2).

Name _____

## Lesson Two        **Worksheet**

*True or False.*

_____ 1. The Apostles' Creed is a summary of what one believes as a Christian believer.

_____ 2. The First Article has nothing to do with personal faith.

_____ 3. "I believe in God..." merely means that I believe in an intellectual way that there is a God.

_____ 4. Faith is personal trust in God through Christ.

_____ 5. The Creed is an expression of a personal relationship to Christ.

_____ 6. If I do not know Christ as my Savior, I cannot truthfully confess the Creed.

_____ 7. If my parents are Christians, then I also am a Christian.

_____ 8. To believe really means to trust, that is, to take God at His Word.

_____ 9. To give mental assent to some fact means to disagree with it.

_____ 10. To believe is to trust with the heart.

_____ 11. Saving faith relies upon Christ for salvation.

_____ 12. It really does not matter what we believe, just as long as we believe.

_____ 13. We believe in the Trinity because the word is found in the Bible.

_____ 14. The Trinity is not very important as far as our salvation is concerned.

_____ 15. The doctrine of the Trinity is found only in the New Testament.

_____ 16. We believe in only one God, but at the same time we believe that this one God consists of the Father, the Son and the Holy Spirit.

_____ 17. If we could understand all that there is to know about God, then we would be like God.

_____ 18. We are not to believe anything that we do not understand.

_____ 19. If we are to learn what God is like, we must go to the Bible.

_____ 20. Because God is a Spirit, we are not able to see Him with our physical eyes.

_____ 21. Because God is a Spirit, He is to be thought of as an imaginary being which exists in our minds.

_____ 22. Because God is holy He also demands that we too be holy.

_____ 23. The fact that God knows all things should be a warning to us against sinning.

_____ 24. We can never be sure that God really loves us.

_____ 25. All the things that God does are good and good for us.

*Completion Questions.*

26. Why is the little word "I" in "I believe..." of the Apostles' Creed so important?

27. To believe really means

to_____with_____,

to_____with_____, and

to_____with_____.

28. What do we mean by the Trinity?

29. Why is the Trinity a necessary part of God's plan of redemption?

30. What does it mean that God is holy?

*Answer the following questions from your study of Acts 2.*

31. What happened on the day of Pentecost?

32. How did the people react to Peter's sermon?

33. How many accepted his message and were added to the church on the day of Pentecost, and what did they devote themselves to?

# God the Father Almighty

*Assignment*

Read Acts 3. Review the First Article and its meaning, and study questions 133-139 in the *Explanation of Luther's Small Catechism*. Read this lesson, complete the worksheet and be prepared for a quiz.

*He who dwells in the shelter of the Most High will rest in the shadow of the Almighty. I will say of the Lord, "He is my refuge and my fortress, my God, in whom I trust." Psalm 91:1-2*

## What Is God Like?

"I believe in God, the Father Almighty, Maker of heaven and earth." In this article three statements are made about God. He is the *Father*, the *Almighty*, and the *Maker of heaven and earth.* They are used in the First Article not to exhaust the full content of the Creed or to give a complete description of God, but to help us know something about the nature of God, that we might come to know Him.

## God the Father

The three persons of the Trinity are equal, without difference in rank or in origin, and all are from eternity. To help us understand God, we speak of the Father as the first person of the Trinity, of the Son as the second person, and of the Holy Spirit as the third person. When the word *Father* is used to address God in our prayers, as for example in the Lord's Prayer, the word refers, not to the first person of the Trinity, but to all three persons as one God. The first person of the Trinity is called the Father, because He is:

1. *The Father of our Lord Jesus Christ.* The word *Father*, as used in speaking of the first person of the Trinity, has a specific meaning, and refers to His relationship to the Son. He is the Father of our Lord Jesus Christ.

2. *The Father of all people, in the sense of creator.* A father brings into being and gives life to his children. Since God has created all people, He is called the Father of all. We read in Malachi 2:10, "Have we not all one Father? Did not one God create us?"

3. *The Father of His children in Jesus Christ.* Through Jesus Christ, He becomes our Father. Faith in Christ brings us into a new relationship in which we enter into a spiritual child relationship to God. A child is permitted to say "Father," and the gift of Jesus Christ makes it possible for us to be children of God.

Therefore, if you are not a Christian, a believer in Christ, you cannot truthfully call God your Father. In Galatians 3:26 we read, "You are all sons of God through faith in Christ Jesus."

God has made known His love to us through His name, Father. It was out of His fatherly love that He sent

His Son, the Lord Jesus Christ, to be our Redeemer. Therefore, the First Article is closely related to the other two articles which speak about redemption and sanctification.

**God Is Almighty**

In the First Article we confess that God is Almighty. As we bring all the teachings in the Bible together about God, we must confess that God is truly Almighty. He is able to do all things. He is able to help us in every time of need.

The fact that God is Almighty assures Christians that God is able to keep and protect them for time and eternity. It is no wonder that we are commanded in the First Commandment, "You shall have no other gods before me."

The fact that God is Almighty is also a stern warning to unrepentant sinners. It reminds them that the day of judgment is coming when God shall judge the lost for having refused to repent and accept His forgiveness in Jesus Christ.

We are all in the hands of the Almighty. Back of all created things stands the living God who has us completely in His power. This thought is comforting if we know Him as our Father and can think of Him as being in a father-child relationship to us. The thought that we are in God's hands is comforting. However, all who do not know Him as Heavenly Father can only await His judgment.

God is called *Almighty* and *Maker* because by His word He made all things out of nothing. He spoke things into being. He said, "Let there be..." and there was. "In the beginning God created the heavens and the earth" (Genesis 1:1).

*The Angels* - The existence of the angels cannot be known from reason or nature, but only from the Bible in the Old and in the New Testaments. They are actual beings and not mere personifications of the attributes of God or of the forces of nature. They are beings of a particular kind. The time of their creation is not known. It must be somewhere within the period described in the first chapter of Genesis, and before God rested on the seventh day.

Why did God create the angels? It is best to say, as in the creation of man, that God created the angels in order that they might share in His life and love. They are His ministering servants and messengers. Their work is to serve God and God's people, the Christians.

*The Nature of Angels* - Angels, like us, are persons, having self-consciousness and self-determination. They think and feel and will. Unlike us, they have no bodies and are pure spirits and, therefore, they are invisible. However, in the history of God's revelation to us, they have assumed bodies in order to be visible to us and to talk with us. Those visible bodies were bodies, just as the angels who appeared to Abraham and Lot in Genesis 18 and 19.

Pictures are meant to visualize certain characteristics of their nature. Wings indicate that angels can move rapidly from one place to another. White garments represent their purity. Sometimes they are referred to as men in order to stress their strength and bravery. They have more knowledge and power than we, but they are nevertheless beings who are far below the greatness of God. The angels are not a race. God created Adam and Eve and told them to increase and replenish the earth. The angels are, however, sexless. They are not male or female, and neither do they marry nor are they given in marriage. (Matthew 22:30).

*Good and Evil Angels* - The angels at their creation were perfect and flawless beings. They were all made holy. Given the freedom of the will as human beings were, they were meant to choose the service of God and to continue in it. Some of the angels used their freedom to serve God and do His will, thus fulfilling the purpose which God had in mind for them. Others, however, misused their freedom and acted against God's will. As a result of this different attitude toward the will of God, the angels now find themselves in two widely different states.

The good angels, because of their constant choice of good, have been confirmed and established in righteousness so that they are no longer able to sin, and cannot fall away from God. The evil angels, who sinned, fell because they wanted to be like God. Satan was an angel of high rank in heaven, but evidently he persuaded many other angels to follow him, and they were all cast out of heaven without hope of redemption.

Satan is a being and not an evil principle in someone or something. He is cunning and powerful and aims his attacks at us as individuals. We cannot overcome him in our own strength, but we can in Jesus. Therefore, "Put on the full armor of God so that you can take your stand against the devil's schemes" (Ephesians 6:11).

# Lesson Three            Worksheet

*True or False.*

_____  1. In the First Article God is spoken of as the Father, Son and Holy Spirit.

_____  2. The First Article gives a complete description of God.

_____  3. The Father is referred to as the first person of the Trinity.

_____  4. The Father has the most important position in the Trinity.

_____  5. When we pray "Our Father" we are really praying to all three persons in the Trinity.

_____  6. Because Jesus is the Son, He is less than the Father.

_____  7. Because God has created all people, He is called the Father of all.

_____  8. Those who do not know Christ as Savior cannot truthfully call God their Heavenly Father.

_____  9. God has made known His love to us through His name, Father.

_____  10. There is no relationship between the three articles of the Apostles' Creed.

_____  11. All the teachings of the Bible indicate that God is truly Almighty.

_____  12. We do not have any assurance that God is able to help us in every time of need.

_____  13. The unrepentant sinners do not need to fear God because He is Almighty.

_____  14. The day of judgment is coming when God will judge the lost for having refused to repent and accept His forgiveness in Jesus Christ.

_____  15. The unbeliever can take comfort in the fact that the Father is Almighty.

_____  16. The angels were not a part of the creative work of God.

_____  17. Reason or nature do not give any evidence for the existence of angels.

_____  18. Angels are not real beings, but are like ghosts.

_____  19. God created the angels to serve Him and share in His love.

_____  20. Angels are persons who think and feel and will as we do.

_____  21. Angels have never been known to be in a visible form.

_____ 22. The angels have families as we do.
_____ 23. The angels at their creation were all perfect and holy beings.
_____ 24. It is still possible for the good angels to fall into sin.
_____ 25. Satan was once a high ranking angel in heaven.

## Completion Questions.

26. What is the First Article of the Apostles' Creed?

27. Who can truthfully call God their Father, and why?

28. Why is the fact that God is Almighty a warning to the unrepentant sinner?

29. What do we know about the nature of angels?

30. Why was Satan cast out of heaven?

## Answer the following questions from your study of Acts 3.

31. What did the crippled man expect to get from Peter and John and what did he get instead?

32. How did Peter say the crippled man had been healed?

33. What did Peter say the people had done with Jesus and what should they have done?

---

# God the Maker of Heaven and Earth

*Assignment*

Read Acts 4. Review the First Article and its meaning, and study questions 140-148 in the *Explanation of Luther's Small Catechism*. Read this lesson, complete the worksheet and be prepared for a quiz.

*Know the Lord is God. It is he who made us, and we are his; we are his people, the sheep of his pasture. Enter his gates with thanksgiving and his courts with praise; give thanks to him and praise His name. Psalm 100:3-4*

## God the Creator

In the Apostles' Creed we confess that we believe in an Almighty God who was also the *Maker* or *Creator* of heaven and earth. The first two chapters of the book of Genesis tell us more about the creation which God has made. The word *create* in the Bible means that God has brought into being, or caused to exist what did not exist before. God created the world out of nothing. We can make things out of materials which already exist, but only God can create things out of materials which did not exist already. In other words, we can make or build, but only God can create.

## The Creation of the Earth

God is the Almighty Maker of all things visible and invisible. He created the heavens and the earth in the six days of creation. On the first day He spoke and there was light. On the second day He created the firmament or the heavens, separating the heavens from the earth. On the third day He created the lands and seas, separating the waters from the land, and the grass, shrubs and trees that covered the earth. On the fourth day He created the sun, moon and stars. On the fifth day He created the fish and the birds. On the sixth day He created the land animals and man. And on the seventh day God rested (Genesis 1,2).

All that the Father does He does through the Son. Therefore, all things were created through the Son, Jesus Christ. God created the world by His Word, that is, through the Word that "was with God," "was God," and "became flesh" (John 1). This means that the Son is its creator, as He is its continual support, its unity and its final purpose. For example, the law of gravity which keeps fixed things in their places and regulates the motion of moving things is an expression of His mind and will. The facts of nature are the acts of God. Visible creation reflects God and points to Him. Apart from Him, creation is an unexplainable riddle.

# The Creation of People

The chief beings which God created are angels and people. The good angels are spirits of light who praise God, carry out His commands, and serve and protect His people. The evil angels are spirits of darkness who fell away from God, oppose His will, tempt people to sin and unbelief, and try to destroy them.

In Genesis 1:27-28 we read about the creation of the human race, "So God created man in his own image, in the image of God he created him; male and female he created them. God blessed them and said to them, 'Be fruitful and increase in number; fill the earth and subdue it. Rule over the fish of the sea and the birds of the air and over every living creature that moves on the ground.'"

People were made in the image of God, so that they were like Him in wisdom and holiness. This refers to a spiritual likeness, not a physical likeness, since God is a spirit and does not have a body. When Adam and Eve fell into sin, however, this image of God was lost. Because the image of God was lost everyone has become darkened in their minds, perverted in their wills, corrupted by sin. The result of this separation from God is death: spiritual death, physical death and eternal death.

These people God created were tested by temptation, in order that they might freely choose to believe God, obey His will, and thus make the truth and goodness of God their own. In unbelief they chose to disobey God and to do their own will. Selfishness became the ruling motive of their hearts. They yielded to the temptation of the serpent, cut themselves off from fellowship with God, lost what they had received, and instead of a blessing, brought down upon themselves and the world the curse of a righteous God. God, however, did not reject them. He planned a way of salvation by promising a Savior to deliver them from sin, death and hell.

## In the Beginning

The Bible tells us that God did all of these things in the beginning. No one knows for certain the time of the beginning. Some say it was millions or even billions of years ago. However, this seems to be an attempt to escape from God and be free from His control altogether, letting nature become "god." Many others say the beginning was about six thousand years ago, based largely upon the genealogical records in the Bible. Recent geological evidence and scientific research increasingly support this view. Those who insist on an ancient beginning because they say science requires it, ask, "Would God deceive us by making things appear to be older than they actually are?" No, not at all. God's purpose was to make things fully functional.

Furthermore, God is able to create anything in the midst of the aging process. We should not limit God by our concept of beginnings. Adam and Eve were brought into being as mature adults. The trees in the Garden of Eden were mature and bearing fruit. In the New Testament, Jesus instantly turned water into wine, which normally required an aging process. Although the Bible does not tell us when all these things came to be, more and more evidence seems to indicate a recent creation.

The important fact to remember is that God created all things. The world, the universe, and all that it contains did not just happen to come into being by itself or by accident. God, in the beginning, made all things. The biblical account leaves no room for any accident in the creation of the world.

## Evolution

You have heard about the theory of origins called *evolution*. The word *evolution* is often used in two ways. Sometimes it is used to refer to gradual changes which have taken place in the earth or the universe since creation. In another way, it is used to set forth the belief that all things, as they exist today, have come into being by a process of evolution. In other words, it says that the human race has evolved from an animal existence, from manlike apes. The view that man has evolved from animals is contrary to the teaching of the Bible.

We cannot answer all questions. The purpose of the Bible is the salvation of our souls. God does want us to know something about creation, but He did not consider it necessary that we should know every detail about it. The Bible is God's revelation of the truth and it must be true and correct since only God has the wisdom to know the absolute truth. Science is human groping for the truth. Science deals with those things which can be measured. However, you cannot find God by using the scientific method. This does not mean that science must deny the existence of God.

You must remember that evolution is a theory and not a proven fact. A theory is a statement which one makes and then tries to prove the truth of it. On the one hand, many scientists have tried to prove the correctness of the evolutionary theory. On the other hand, there are many other scientists today who are willing to accept the biblical account of creation and who work within that framework of belief.

## How Long Did Creation Take?

Another question to which we have no final answer is, "How long did God take to create all things?" Various explanations have been given to the meaning of the word *day* as it is used in Genesis 1 and 2. Some say, because the Hebrew is a more figurative language than most, it refers to long periods of time, as the word is often used in the Old Testament. However, others insist it means a twenty-four hour day. It seems hard to escape the conviction that these were ordinary days when we read the almost monotonous repetition of evening and morning. Are we to believe that the sun continued to shine for thousands of years without setting? Notice also that the plants were created on the third day, while the sun was created on the fourth day. It would be possible for the plants to exist one day without the sun, but not for a long period of time (Genesis 1:3-2:2).

After the six days of creation, God rested on the seventh day and commanded that the Jews were also to rest on the seventh day. Certainly they were not required to rest for an era, or a long period of time, but for a day (Exodus 20:8-11; Exodus 31:16-18). Whenever the Hebrew word for day is used with a definite number, it always means a literal day of twenty-four hours. The insistence upon an ancient earth and days as long periods of time is because the theory of evolution demands it. We must remember that it was God who created all things. God is Almighty. He could do it in any way He pleased.

# Lesson Four          Worksheet

*True or False.*

_____ 1. When we speak of our existence, we begin with ourselves.

_____ 2. The first two chapters of Matthew tell us about the creation God made.

_____ 3. God created the world out of nothing.

_____ 4. People have created many beautiful things.

_____ 5. God called all things into being by just speaking words.

_____ 6. God created the heavens and the earth in seven days.

_____ 7. All that the Father does, He does through the Son.

_____ 8. The Word that "was with God" and "became flesh" refers to Jesus Christ.

_____ 9. The laws of nature give us an expression of the mind and will of God.

_____ 10. Creation can easily be explained apart from Jesus Christ.

_____ 11. The revelation of God in His Word is centered in Jesus Christ.

_____ 12. We were created in the image of God, spiritually, physically and emotionally.

_____ 13. We have retained, or kept, the image of God.

_____ 14. The result of our fall into sin is death.

_____ 15. The people God created were tested by temptation, in order that they might choose freely to believe God and obey His will.

_____ 16. Selfishness is the ruling motive of our hearts.

_____ 17. God does not want to have anything more to do with us because Adam and Eve sinned against Him.

_____ 18. The Bible clearly tells us the time when all things came to be.

_____ 19. According to the Bible, things did not just come into being by accident.

_____ 20. Evolution can refer to the gradual changes which have taken place in the earth or universe since creation.

_____ 21. Recent geological evidence indicates more and more that creation is millions of years old.

_____ 22. The final purpose of the Bible is the salvation of our souls.

_____ 23. The Bible is God's revelation of the truth and it must be true and correct since only God has the wisdom to know the absolute truth.

_____ 24. That human beings evolved from animals is a theory and not a proven fact.

_____ 25. We know all things were created in days consisting of twenty-four hours.

*Completion Questions.*

26. What does the word "create" mean?

27. What did God make on each of the days of creation?

First Day _____ Fourth Day _____

Second Day _____ Fifth Day _____

Third Day _____ Sixth Day _____

28. Explain the theory of evolution.

29. Describe the relationship between the Bible and truth, and science and truth.

*Answer the following questions from your study of Acts 4.*

30. Why did the Sadducees have Peter and John put in jail?

31. Why did Peter and John say they could not stop teaching in Jesus' name?

32. How did the Christians in the early church respond to the needy?

# God the Preserver and Provider

## Assignment

Read Acts 5 and 6. Review the First Article and its meaning, and study questions 149-156 in the *Explanation of Luther's Small Catechism*. Read this lesson, complete the worksheet and be prepared for a quiz.

*And my God will meet all your needs according to his glorious riches in Christ Jesus. Philippians 4:19*

### God My Creator

"I believe in God, the Father Almighty, Maker of heaven and earth." The *Explanation* says this means, "I believe that God has created me and all that exists. He has given to me and still sustains my body and soul, my senses and all my members, my reason and all the powers of my soul." This Article tells us that God provides and cares for all that He has created, especially for people, and most of all for His believing children. This is called the providence of God and is shown in His support of His creation, in His government of the world, and in His directing all things toward His divine goal.

In our last lesson we learned that God is the Almighty Maker of all things visible and invisible. There are three orders of creatures which God has made.

1) The animals, which are all body and have no soul.
2) The angels, which are all soul and have no body.
3) And people, which have both body and soul.

Of all these creatures, the human race was God's main creation. In Genesis we are told that God made people in His own image. In their original state they were good in every respect. They had no sin or natural desire to sin. They, like God, were able to make right choices and decisions. Their minds were enlightened so that they knew God and His works. Their will and the desire of their hearts was holy and in harmony with God's will. They wanted to do God's will. Their consciences were full of peace and joy and free from sin and guilt. The physical condition of their bodies was also perfect and free from disease, fear and worry.

## The Fall

In Genesis, chapter 3, we learn that this perfect man and woman did not remain perfect for long. God did not create them like robots to do whatever He dictated. Instead, He gave them a free will which allowed them the ability to choose and make decisions. God's purpose and desire was that people would use this will to serve Him and live for Him. However, a will that is free to decide for God can also be used against God. In other words, a free will has the ability to obey or to disobey. Otherwise there is no choice, or in reality, no free will. It was then that the devil tempted Eve to doubt what God had said about the Tree of Knowledge. When Eve yielded to temptation and gave of the forbidden fruit to Adam, and he ate of it, they rebelled against God and lost the perfection with which they were created. This act of rebellion by Adam and Eve is called the *Fall*. Thus sin entered into the world, because they abused their freedom and set up their own wills against God's will. Ever since that time every person is born separated from God. The natural desire of every human is to turn away from God and to rebel against Him. Not all people express this rebellion in the same awful ways but all people possess the natural desire to do so.

## All Things Good at Creation

All things as they came from the hand of God were good. "God saw all that he had made, and it was very good" (Genesis 1:31). There was no sin in the world. All that God created was free from every defect or evil of any kind. But sin entered into the world and all people by nature became sinful. Still, the human body is a wonderful gift from God and is not sinful in itself. It is the soul that has natural sinful desires. The soul includes the reason and the faculties of the mind, the invisible and immortal self, a person's real self. The soul is the immaterial part of a person which inhabits and moves the body. The body, therefore, becomes an organ of sin only when so used by the soul. Sin is a defect, not in matter, but in the will. We should always remember that it is not the body which is sinful, but the thoughts and desires that direct the body.

The origin of sin, as we have already seen, is not to be traced to God as its author, but to Satan who used the self-determination of the beings God made. God did not create sinful beings, and neither did He plan or intend that any of them should sin. Rather, He desired that all His creatures should live in perfect fellowship with Him. Sin came into the world because Adam and Eve by their own voluntary act turned away from God and listened to the devil. First came the self-originated sin of the devil. Then came their sin when they yielded to the temptation of the devil.

Some think that eating the forbidden fruit is too small a thing to have brought such terrible consequences into the world. It was no small thing, however, because by it Adam and Eve set up their own wills in opposition to God's will. In defiance of God we, too, have set out for ourselves on a path of our own choosing. God is a just God and any act of disobedience, great or small, is such that it brings us under His judgment.

## God My Father

By act of creation God is the Father of all people in the sense that He is the Creator. This, however, does not mean that all people are living in a saving relationship with God as their personal heavenly Father.

God becomes your heavenly Father when you come to trust His Son, the Lord Jesus Christ. You become a child of God when you receive Jesus Christ into your life as your Savior from sin. Only then do you become a child of God. If you were baptized as an infant, God received you into his family in spite of the fact that you were born a sinner. Unfortunately, many baptized children, when they become adolescents, turn away from the Lord and rebel against the God who loved them. Yet, like the father in the story of the prodigal son (Luke 15), God is ready to receive back all those who repent of their sin and trust in Jesus for salvation. Only then can you call God your heavenly Father. Since God is the Father of Jesus Christ, God becomes your heavenly Father through Jesus. Sons and daughters call their earthly fathers, "father," because of their relationship with him. Likewise, you can call God your heavenly Father only through a relationship with Christ. This means that God is not your heavenly Father unless you have received Jesus Christ as your Savior.

## God My Provider

In the explanation to the First Article, Martin Luther gave his own testimony about his heavenly Father, as found in the *Small Catechism*, "I believe that He gives me food and clothing, home and family, and all material blessings; that He daily provides abundantly for all the needs of my life, protects me from all danger, and guards and keeps me from all evil..."

God cares for all that He has made. He provides for all our daily needs. He protects you from earthly dangers on every hand and shields you against every spiritual evil. He gives you grace to endure every trial and difficulty. He also directs the course of history according to His plan of salvation. All this He does because He is your Father and loves you as His child by faith in Christ.

God is a good God. He provides many blessings, and He pours them out richly upon all people, whether they have become His children through faith in Jesus Christ or not. Even the wicked and those who are unthankful are objects of His goodness. They receive many temporal benefits from Him even though they refuse to accept His spiritual gifts. When I truly come to know Him as my Father, then I can accept these gifts with a sense of thanksgiving in my heart. All too often people accept these gifts as if they really deserved them and as if they had earned them entirely by themselves. God does not really owe us anything except hell. This is because we have all "sinned and (fallen) short of the glory of God" (Romans 3:23).

As Martin Luther looked back upon the experiences of his life he could truly testify how God had protected him many times when he faced danger. God may allow many trials to come our way but the person who knows God as his Father can trust Him to protect and guard him from every evil.

God preserves our earthly life by means of the gifts He has given to us. Among these gifts is our ability to think. Food, clothing, home and family, and all our property are also gifts which God gives for the maintenance of life. Our lives bear witness to the goodness of God who desires to give all these gifts to His own.

## My Response

Again, Martin Luther states in his testimony about his heavenly Father, that there should be a daily response to God. "All this He does because of His fatherly and divine goodness and mercy, without any merit or worthiness in me. For all this I should thank, praise, serve and obey Him. This is most certainly true."

When I trust in Jesus Christ as my Savior, I am a child of God. Then I can truly say the First Article as a real confession of faith, "I believe in God, the Father Almighty, Maker of heaven and earth."

# Lesson Five     **Worksheet**

*True or False.*

_____  1. God cares most for people and especially His believing children.

_____  2. Angels are creatures which are all body and have no soul.

_____  3. The book of Matthew tells us about the creation of man and woman.

_____  4. In their original state, human beings were like God—good in every respect.

_____  5. When human beings were created they wanted to do God's will and do what was right.

_____  6. In the beginning human beings were perfect physically as well as spiritually.

_____  7. God created human beings like robots who would do whatever they were told to do.

_____  8. It was God's purpose and desire that we should serve Him and live for Him.

_____  9. A person with a free will has the ability only to choose against God.

_____  10. The devil first tempted Adam to doubt what God had said about the Tree of Knowledge, and when he ate of the forbidden fruit, he gave it to Eve.

_____  11. Adam and Eve rebelled against God and lost the perfection with which they had been created.

_____  12. Sin entered into the world because people set up their own will instead of God's will as their standard.

_____  13. The natural desire of people today is to go to God.

_____  14. It is not the body which is sinful but the natural desires of the soul.

_____  15. God is the author of sin because He permitted Adam and Eve to sin.

_____  16. The first act of sin in God's creation was committed by Adam and Eve..

_____  17. God will overlook some acts of disobedience because He is a God of love.

_____  18. By the act of creation, God is the Father of all people.

19. Since God created all people, all are living in a saving relationship with God.

20. God is not your heavenly Father unless you have received Jesus Christ as your personal Savior.

21. God protects us from earthly dangers and shields us against spiritual evil.

22. God blesses only those who have become His children through faith in Christ.

23. God does not owe us anything except hell.

24. Only some people have sinned and fallen short of the glory of God.

25. Our daily response to our heavenly Father should be one of thanksgiving.

*Completion Questions.*

26. What do we mean by the providence of God?

27. What is the difference between the three orders of creatures God has made?

   a.
   b.
   c.

28. What is meant by a free will?

29. Why was the eating of the forbidden fruit by Adam and Eve such a great sin?

30. How may God be your heavenly Father?

*Answer the following questions from your study of Acts 5 and 6.*

31. Why did Ananias and Sapphira die?

32. Record Peter's answer to the captain of the temple when he was told, "Not to teach in this name."

33. Why did the twelve apostles choose others to care for the widows and the poor?

# The Lord Jesus Christ

## *Assignment*

Read Acts 7. Memorize the Second Article and its meaning, and study questions 157-159 in the *Explanation of Luther's Small Catechism*. Read this lesson, complete the worksheet and be prepared for a quiz.

*To all who received him, to those who believed in His name, he gave the right to become children of God. John 1:12*

## Christ's Work of Redemption

"I believe in Jesus Christ, His only Son, our Lord, who was conceived by the Holy Spirit, born of the Virgin Mary, suffered under Pontius Pilate, was crucified, dead and buried; He descended into hell; the third day He rose again from the dead; He ascended into heaven, and is seated at the right hand of God the Father Almighty; from whence He shall come to judge the living and the dead."

The Second Article speaks of God the Son and His work of redemption. This article states the main events in

Christ's work of redeeming us. The article ends with a statement about His coming again at the end of the age.

## "I Believe"

The Second Article begins with the words "I believe...," just as the First Article on God the Father begins with these same words. The creed begins this way because the Apostles' Creed is a summary of what one believes as a Christian. Therefore, we do not say "We believe," but "I believe." It is the confession of a personal faith. Only as you accept Jesus Christ as your Savior and trust in Him as your Lord, can you truthfully say the Second Article.

To believe is not merely to know certain facts with the mind and to agree with them. It is also to commit oneself to those facts and to trust in them. For example, you may believe the ice is strong enough to hold you up. However, if you are not willing to step out and walk on that ice, to put your trust in it, you really do not believe it will hold you up. Many know and believe that Jesus is the Savior of the world, but they have not put their trust in Him. They have not committed themselves to Him. In John 1:12 we read that to believe in Him is to receive Him. Are you living in daily repentance and faith? Then you can honestly give the Second Article as your own testimony.

## Our Need

The sinful and lost condition in which we find ourselves because of our sinful nature is one from which we cannot free ourselves by any possible means. We are guilty and deserve condemnation at the hands of a just and holy God. We are spiritually helpless, unable to serve God by our own natural powers. We are unable to do anything to free ourselves from the guilt or the bondage of sin. If we are to be saved, it must be by God's grace alone. This grace is offered to all people in Christ, the Redeemer (Titus 2:11).

## God's Saving Love

Salvation is a revelation of the loving heart of God. Moved with compassion, God planned from all eternity to send His only begotten Son into the world to redeem us. God's plan to save us was made when He planned to create us. Since God knew beforehand that we would sin, our creation cannot be understood apart from the eternal purpose of God to redeem us. In the Old Testament, God promised to deliver people from sin and its awful consequences. This promise was first given to Adam and Eve in the Garden of Eden. In Genesis 3:15, God said to the serpent, "And I will put enmity between you and the woman, and between your offspring and hers; he will crush your head and you will strike his heel." The offspring of the woman, which here refers to Christ, will crush or defeat the serpent's head, which refers to the devil. Later this promise was given to Abraham in Genesis 12:3, "All peoples on earth will be blessed through you." It was also given to Isaac in Genesis 26:4, to Jacob in Genesis 28:14, to David in II Samuel 7:16, and the prophets. "Therefore the Lord himself will give you a sign: The virgin will be with child and will give birth to a son, and will call him Immanuel" (Isaiah 7:14). Christ's coming fulfilled this promise.

## Jesus Christ, God's Son

In the New Testament it says, "When the time had fully come, God sent his Son, born of a woman, born under law, to redeem those under law, that we might receive the full rights of son" (Galatians 4:4-5). To save us, the Son of God, the second person of the Triune God, became a human being. As a man, He became our substitute for the penalty of our sin. He had a human body. He grew from babyhood into an adult human being. As a human being, he suffered human wants such as hunger, thirst, weariness and pain (Matthew 4:12). He was moved by human emotions, such as joy, sorrow and indignation (Luke 10:21, Matthew 26:38). He wept (John 11:35). He prayed (Matthew 26:39). He suffered and died (I Peter 2:23-24). He could not have done any of these things if He had not been a human being such as we are. The word *coming*, in reference to Christ, implies pre-existence, which means that He existed before He was born on earth as a man.

Martin Luther said, "The sum of this article is the little word 'Lord.' It means that Christ has redeemed me from sin, from the devil, from death and all misery. For before, I had no Lord and King but was captive under the devil's power. ... Thus all the tyrants and oppressors have been routed, and in their stead is Jesus Christ, the Lord of life, of righteousness, of everything pertaining to my welfare and salvation. He has rescued us poor lost creatures from the jaws of hell; He has redeemed us, made us free, and restored us to God's favor and grace; He has taken us as His own, under His shelter and protection, that under His government we may experience His mercy, His power and wisdom, His life and salvation" (*A Study Course in*

*Luther's Small Catechism* by C. J. Sodergren, Augsburg Publishing House, Minneapolis, pp. 55, 56, 1936).

All who can say "Jesus is Lord," and can put themselves under the lordship of Jesus, can say the creed. Even though other statements in the creed may be hard to understand, this one is not. Here is a confession of Christ who, as our Lord, has delivered us from the bondage of sin.

## The Eternal Purpose of God

It is God's will or purpose that all people should live in fellowship with Him. This is why God created us. Even when we sin and separate ourselves from God, God in His eternal purpose has provided a way of salvation by which we can be brought back into fellowship with Him. The eternal purpose of God offers salvation to all.

The purpose of God to save us is eternal. It was first announced after the fall in Eden, but it was not formed then. Redemption is not an afterthought by which God planned to repair as best He could the damage done by the fall into sin. God foreknew we would sin. From eternity He determined to save us. The purpose to create us and the purpose to redeem us were co-eternal in the mind of God.

The purpose of God to save us is a free act of His divine grace. There is nothing in us to deserve such treatment. Rather, by our sin we justly deserve punishment and eternal separation from God's presence. The love of God, however, is so great that it moved Him to do all that was within His almighty power to rescue us. Therefore, He sent His Son to redeem us. He earnestly seeks through the work of the Holy Spirit to bring us to faith in Christ.

The purpose of God to save us is universal. That is, it includes all people. "God wants all men to be saved and to come to a knowledge of the truth" (I Timothy 2:4). "He is patient with you, not wanting anyone to perish, but everyone to come to repentance" (II Peter 3:9). Jesus died for all, for the sins of the whole world.

The purpose of God is to save those who believe in Christ. It is not a plan to save all people regardless of their attitude toward Christ. While salvation is offered to all, it is actually possessed only by those who receive it by faith. It is only by faith that the merits of Christ are received and become ours personally. It is God's will to save us from our sins, that is, from the guilt and from the love of sin. Salvation is a deliverance from the guilt and power of sin through faith in Christ. He desires to make us new creatures fitted for eternal life and eternal fellowship with God.

## Our Response

Because Jesus Christ, God's only begotten Son, has done everything for my salvation, only as I allow Him to be my personal Savior and trust in Him, can I be saved. This is an ongoing, daily experience. "Salvation is found in no one else, for there is no other name under heaven given to men by which we must be saved" (Acts 4:12).

Name _____

# Lesson Six          Worksheet

*True or False*

_____ 1. The Second Article speaks of God the Father and His work of redemption.

_____ 2. The Second Article ends with a brief statement about the death of Christ.

_____ 3. The Apostles' Creed is a summary of what one believes as a Christian.

_____ 4. Even the unsaved can truthfully say the Second Article.

_____ 5. To believe also includes the will, that is, to act upon what one knows.

_____ 6. Many people believe that Jesus is the Savior of the world, but they do not personally know Him as their Savior.

_____ 7. If we try hard enough we can free ourselves from the bondage of sin.

_____ 8. We deserve to be condemned by God.

_____ 9. We can be saved by God's grace alone.

_____ 10. God offers His grace only to those who will receive it.

_____ 11. Salvation is a revelation of the loving heart of God.

_____ 12. God planned to save us after the fall into sin in the Garden of Eden.

_____ 13. The first promise in the Old testament of the coming of the Savior was made to Abraham.

_____ 14. Because Jesus was God, He did not experience such human wants as hunger, thirst, weariness or pain.

_____ 15. Jesus became man in order to become our substitute for the penalty of sin.

_____ 16. The sum of the Second Article is found in the little word "Lord. "

_____ 17. We must be able to understand everything in the creed before we can say it.

_____ 18. It is God's will that all people should live in fellowship with Him.

_____ 19. From eternity God planned to send His Son to redeem us.

59

_____ 20. The Holy Spirit has no part in bringing us to true faith in Christ.

_____ 21. God's plan of redemption was merely an afterthought by which He decided to repair as best He could the damage done by the fall into sin.

_____ 22. The plan of God to save us is a free act of His divine grace.

_____ 23. God wants all people to be saved and come to the knowledge of the truth.

_____ 24. God will save all people regardless of their attitude toward Christ.

_____ 25. It is God's will to save us from our sin, from the guilt and love of sin.

*Completion Questions.*

26. Why does the Second Article begin with the words "I believe ... "?

27. Why can we not be saved by our own natural powers?

28. Explain these words, "The offspring of the woman will crush the serpent's head. "

29. Why did Jesus have to become a human being?

30. What is the eternal purpose of God?

*Answer the following questions from your study of Acts 7.*

31. What message did God give Moses from the burning bush?

32. What did Stephan see as he looked up to heaven?

33. What did Stephen pray for just before he was stoned to death?

# The Natures of Christ

## Assignment

Read Acts 8. Review the Second Article and its meaning, and study questions 160-168 in the *Explanation of Luther's Small Catechism*. Read this lesson, complete the worksheet and be prepared for a quiz.

*The Word became flesh and lived for a while among us. We have seen his glory, the glory of the one and only Son, who came from the Father, full of grace and truth. John 1:14*

### The Second Article of the Apostles' Creed

"I believe in Jesus Christ, His only Son, our Lord, who was conceived by the Holy Spirit, born of the Virgin Mary, suffered under Pontius Pilate, was crucified, dead and buried; He descended into hell; the third day He rose again from the dead; He ascended into heaven, and is seated at the right hand of God the Father Almighty; from whence He shall come to judge the living and the dead."

The explanation to the Second Article says, "I believe that Jesus Christ, true God, begotten of the Father from eternity, and also true man, born of the Virgin Mary, is my Lord..."

The Bible clearly tells us that Jesus Christ was also a human being. "Since the children have flesh and blood, he too shared in their humanity so that by His death He might destroy him who holds the power of death—that is, the devil—and free those who all their lives were held in slavery by their fear of death" (Hebrews 2:14-15).

## A Unique Person

Jesus Christ was a unique person. From the Bible we learn that He possessed two natures. The one nature was *divine* and the other nature was *human.* From John 1:1-3, and other passages, we learn that the Son of God has always been. The divine nature of Jesus never had a beginning. He has always been. It is not until He was born in Bethlehem that we read of His becoming *flesh*, that is a *human being* (John 1:14). The human nature, then, did have a beginning. It began with His conception in the womb of the Virgin Mary. It was then that the Son of God became a human being.

Jesus claimed to be equal with the Father (John 10:10). We are told that we are to honor Jesus as we honor the Father (John 5:23). The Apostle Thomas spoke of Jesus as his Lord and his God (John 20:28). Jesus claimed to be before Abraham (John 8:58). The purpose of His coming into the world was to save sinners (I Timothy 1:15). The saving power of Christ's suffering and death lie in the fact that Jesus was and is God, who in His human nature, died for us.

# Jesus, The God-Man

As we have just seen, the Bible portrays Jesus Christ as both God and man. The divine and human natures are united in Jesus Christ with both natures forming one undivided and indivisible person. There are not two Christs, but only one Christ. The Son of God, who has the divine nature from the beginning, took the human nature into His divine nature when He was conceived of the Holy Spirit in the womb of the Virgin Mary. At one and the same time Jesus Christ is both God and man. The Bible clearly teaches this truth. We must be alert for those religious groups which refuse to believe that Jesus is both God and man.

There are in Christ two natures, the divine and the human. He is true God, and possesses the eternal divine nature of God the Father. He is also true man born of the Virgin Mary and possesses a human nature since the Incarnation. He is as completely God as is God the Father, and He is as completely a human being as we are. That He is truly human is evident from the Gospels. That He is true God is evident from His life and works, from what He says of Himself, and from what His Apostles say of Him.

Just how this can be will always be a deep mystery to us in this world. The only way to understand it lies in making a clear distinction between person and nature, and to think of Christ as one person with two natures, divine and human. The unity of the person is the key to any understanding that is possible for us to have of Christ. He is true God and true man; however, He is only one person, not two persons.

Christ is a divine person with a divine nature from all eternity. But from the time of His incarnation, His birth,

He was a divine person with both a divine and a human nature. "The Word was made flesh" (John 1:14). God became man. At His birth, Christ did not add to Himself a human person but only a human nature. He became man, He did not take possession of a man, nor enter into a man. He did not cease to be the Son of God nor lose or lay aside His divine nature and attributes. But remaining God, He also became man. The person of Christ, who functioned from eternity through a divine intellect and a divine will, began with the Incarnation to function also through a human intellect, a human will and a human body. This union of the divine and human natures in one person is a deep mystery, but it is true.

## The Divine Nature

Christ has a true divine nature. As the Son of God, begotten of the Father, He has the same divine life as God. The Father and the Son are not identical. The Bible makes a distinction between the two, but they are the same divine being. The deity, or the Godhead of the Son, is the same as that of the Father. "God was in Christ," (II Corinthians 5:19, New American Standard Bible). All of God exists and is shown in Christ. Through Him we come to God. In Him we find God. If we pass Him by or leave Him out, we have no God. To believe in Jesus is to believe in God.

## The Human Nature

Christ has a true human nature, with body and soul. He was born of a woman. Like other children, He grew up, became hungry and thirsty, became tired and slept, was tempted, suffered and died. He had human attributes, wants and feelings. Some of the characteristics of Christ's human nature are as follows:

1. His human nature has no separate personality of its own. The personality of Christ is His whole being, including His human nature. There is one divine person functioning through both natures.

2. His human nature is true and complete. Christ is a true human being except that He is without sin. "We have one who has been tempted in every way, just as we are--yet was without sin (Hebrews 4:15b). When Christ was born as a man, He did not take on a human body only, for humanity does not consist only of a body, but of soul and body. Therefore, Christ assumed both a body and a soul.

3. His human nature partook of the natural weaknesses of the human race. The fact that Jesus was God and not born after the common way of nature lifted Him above all the infirmities which come as a result of sin. He voluntarily took upon Himself natural human weaknesses, and became in all things tempted as we are.

4. There was in Christ no *original sin*. *Original sin* is the result of our descent from Adam and Eve. Christ's birth was miraculous in that He had no human father, but only a human mother. He was born without that natural inherited corruption because He was conceived by the Holy Spirit and not by the union of a man and a woman. Having God alone for His Father, He was born a sinless being.

5. There was in Christ no *actual sin.* In the midst of a sinful world, the Bible tells us He lived a perfect life in love to God and to man. His life as a human being was

free from every blemish and fault. "He committed no sin" (I Peter 2:22).

6. Christ could not sin. Since sin is a personal matter and Christ is divine, the question about whether He could sin or not is really a question if God can sin or not. Of course God cannot sin. Therefore Christ could not sin.

7. The body of Jesus was in itself immortal. He died, not as a result of any natural susceptibility to death, but of His own choice. His death was the laying down of His life by Himself, and not the taking it away by others. See John 10:18.

## Why Must Jesus be Both God and Man?

If Jesus was to be our Savior and unite us with God, He had to take upon Himself the nature of both God and man. To accomplish our redemption He must obey, without sin, in all things where we had sinned by our disobedience. This required a human nature. As a member of our race He did what we failed to do, and what we were neither able nor willing to do, that is, to obey God in all things. This He did as man, freely and voluntarily, in our place and for our sake. He could not have been tempted if He had been only God. If He had been only man, He would have gone down in defeat. His life and death would have been a failure. But as the God-Man, Jesus Christ did accomplish our redemption, and whoever receives Him by faith as Savior, can say, "My Lord, who has redeemed me."

# Lesson Seven          Worksheet

*True or False.*

_____ 1. The Second Article tells us only about the divine nature of Christ.

_____ 2. The Bible does not clearly say that Jesus was a human being.

_____ 3. In the Gospel of John we learn that the Son of God has always existed.

_____ 4. Jesus Christ came into being at the Incarnation, that is, His birth.

_____ 5. The divine nature of Jesus never had a beginning.

_____ 6. Jesus never claimed to be equal with the Father.

_____ 7. The purpose of Jesus' coming into the world was to save sinners.

_____ 8. If Jesus was not God, His suffering and death would not have any saving power.

_____ 9. The Son of God took the human nature into His divine nature when He was conceived by the Holy Spirit in the womb of the Virgin Mary.

_____ 10. All religious groups believe that Jesus is both God and man.

_____ 11. Because Jesus is the Son of God, He cannot be true God.

_____ 12. Jesus is as completely God as is God the Father, and He is as completely human as we are.

_____ 13. The life and works of Jesus give evidence that He is true God.

_____ 14. The natures of Christ will always be a deep mystery to us in this world.

_____ 15. Because Jesus is both human and divine, He is two persons.

_____ 16. At His birth, Christ did not add to Himself a human person, but only a human nature.

_____ 17. When Jesus became human, He laid aside His divine nature and attributes, and took possession of a man.

_____ 18. The Father and the Son are identical.

_____ 19. All of God exists and is shown in Christ.

_____ 20. If we pass Christ by, or leave Him out, we have no God.

_____ 21. To believe in Jesus is to believe in God.

_____ 22. Because Jesus is God, He never became tired or tempted as other people.

_____ 23. Original sin is the result of our descent from Adam.

_____ 24. Christ could not sin.

_____ 25. Jesus did not have to be both God and man to be our Redeemer.

*Completion Questions.*

26. How is Jesus Christ a unique person?

27. How can we know that Jesus is truly human and also truly God?

28. As a human being, how is Christ like us and how is He different from us?

29. Why was there no original sin in Christ?

30. Why must Jesus be both God and human?

*Answer the following questions from your study of Acts 8.*

31. Describe what Saul was doing to the Christians?

32. What was Peter's response when Simon offered money to buy the gift of the Spirit?

33. Why did the Lord tell Philip to leave Samaria and go down to Gaza?

# The Offices of Christ

## *Assignment*

Read Acts 9. Review the Second Article and its meaning, and study questions 166-174 in the *Explanation of Luther's Small Catechism*. Read this lesson, complete the worksheet and be prepared for a quiz.

*Therefore since we have a great high priest who has gone through the heavens, Jesus the Son of God, let us hold firmly to the faith we profess. For we do not have a high priest who is unable to sympathize with our weaknesses, but we have one who has been tempted in every way, just as we are--yet was without sin. Hebrews 4:14,15*

### The Second Article of the Apostle's Creed

"I believe in Jesus Christ, His only Son our Lord, who was conceived by the Holy Spirit, born of the Virgin Mary, suffered under Pontius Pilate, was crucified, dead and buried; He descended into hell; the third day He arose again from the dead; He ascended into heaven and is seated at the right hand of God the Father Almighty; from whence He shall come to judge the living and the dead."

## The Names of Christ

The Bible uses various names when it speaks of the Son of God. In the New Testament, His names are given as Jesus Christ or Christ Jesus.

*Jesus is His personal name.* - It is the Greek form of the Hebrew *Joshua* and means *Savior.* This name was given to the Son of God even before He was born. In Matthew 1:21, we read the words spoken to Joseph by an angel of the Lord, "She will give birth to a son, and you are to give him the name Jesus, because he will save his people from their sins." Then in Matthew 1:25 we read, "And he (Joseph) gave Him the name Jesus."

There are many saviors. Doctors save lives; lawyers save their client's name and reputation; and lifeguards save life. But Jesus saves "his people from their sins." The first Joshua defeated the Israelites' enemies. The second and greater Joshua, that is Christ, delivered His people from their more terrible spiritual enemies, and destroyed him that has the power of death, that is the devil. The first Joshua passed over the Jordan and divided the land of promise among the tribes. The second Joshua passed through the cold waters of death and opened the heavenly Canaan to His people, and ascended on high to prepare a place for them in heaven.

Jesus was the personal name by which He was known to His disciples. This name was also placed above Him on the cross. Matthew 27:37 records the words on the cross as, "This is Jesus, the King of the Jews." Artists who have understood the true meaning of the life of Christ have painted the Christ-child, lying in a cradle, with the vision of the cross over His head. This is in recognition of the fact that from earliest childhood Jesus always thought of the cross as His goal in life. He meant to crown His life by dying on the cross. This is revealed in the angel's message to Joseph, "You are to give Him the name *Jesus,* because He will *save...*"

*Christ is His official name.* - It is the Greek form of the Hebrew *Messiah* and means *The Anointed One.* This name also means the promised Savior who has been promised through the Old Testament writers. For this reason Andrew said "...We have found the Messiah" (that is, the Christ) (John 1:41). The woman at the well of Sychar knew something about this too, when she said, "I know that Messiah (called Christ) is coming. When He comes, He will explain everything to us" (John 4:25).

*Christ* is not really a name, but a title which refers to the office He holds, and in which He works, such as that of the president of the United States. The President is sometimes spoken of as *The President of the United States.* President is his official name and it speaks of his office. So it is with the Son of God. It is the office of Christ which He holds and through which He works. The Bible makes it clear that it is Jesus who was born of the Virgin Mary, who is also the Christ, the promised Savior spoken of in the Old Testament.

In the Old Testament, priests and kings were anointed. Aaron and his sons were anointed. Some prophets were anointed. Elijah anointed Elisha. Samuel anointed Saul, that is, he poured oil over his head. By this sign all the people knew that Saul was chosen for the work of a king. Today, however, kings are usually crowned. Christ was also anointed, not with oil, but with the Holy Spirit at the time of His baptism. In this way He was chosen or set apart for a specific work—a threefold work.

## The Threefold Office of Christ

*Office* means a position of authority. When we study the Bible, we find that the office of Christ has three specific functions. Each office also gives us a different aspect or view of Christ and His work.

*Prophet* - Jesus Christ came to teach us God's will. A prophet is one who speaks for another. A prophet of God is one who speaks for God, making known and interpreting the Word and the will of God to the people. The office of a prophet, then, is not simply that of predicting future events but of proclaiming God's will to men. The main work of the Old Testament prophets was to call people to repentance by the sincere preaching of the Law and to faith by the proclamation of the coming redemption. They certainly did at times predict future events.

The main work of Christ as a prophet was to proclaim the Gospel, to announce the coming of the kingdom of God, to tell us about the love of God and the way we might come to God and be saved. It is a kingdom into which all are invited and urged to enter. We can enter this kingdom only by undergoing a change of mind, by becoming converted, by being born again. This change happens by the means of God's grace. Unless there is a complete inner change of attitude toward sin and God, we cannot become or remain a member of the kingdom. Christ Himself is the founder and center of this kingdom. He said, "I am the way and the truth and the life. No one comes to the Father except through me" (John 14:6).

The prophetic office of Christ did not end with His ministry on earth, but is still carried on today by His servants who proclaim His Word for Him and in His place. He will carry out that office through the church until the end of the world. It is through them that Christ continues His work as prophet. This makes the gospel ministry the highest and most responsible office in the world.

*Priest* - As a priest, Jesus Christ came to atone for our sins and to pray for us. A priest is one who makes sacrifices for sin and offers prayer to God on behalf of others. As a priest, Jesus Christ made one great sacrifice for all the sins of the world. This was by His own death upon the cross.

In the accomplishment of our salvation Christ is our great High Priest, who as the mediator between us and God, has satisfied in full for us all the demands of God's law and prays for us. The priests of the Old Testament brought a sacrifice for sin, whereas Christ not only brought a sacrifice but was Himself the sacrifice.

The priestly work of Christ naturally falls into two parts, namely *satisfaction* and *intercession*. It is called a satisfaction because in His suffering and death Jesus has satisfied for us all the demands of God's Law. The Law demands that we are to be perfectly righteous in thought, word and deed. The Law demands that we be punished for every sin. Since all have sinned and come short of the glory of God, and since by nature we lack the righteousness which we should have before God, we deserve to be punished. However much God in His love wanted to save us, it was not possible for Him to do so unless God's law was satisfied. Therefore, Jesus became human, in order that He might fulfill all the holy demands of the law for us and might bear for us all, by His death upon the cross, the penalty which we deserved because of our sins. The second part of Christ's priestly work is His intercession.

Now that He has been raised from the dead and ascended to heaven, He lives to pray for us continually.

*King* - As a king, Jesus Christ is to reign over us now. He is also to reign over us in the future when He returns in power and great glory. A king is one who has power and authority to rule over a people within a kingdom.

Christ has been crowned as the Ruler over all things, especially over the Christian Church. As king He rules over the Kingdom of Power, that is, the world or the entire creation. He also rules over the Kingdom of Grace, that is, the church or all who from the heart believe in Him as Savior and Lord.

And finally He rules over the Kingdom of Glory— that is, heaven. Only as we by faith in Christ become members of Christ's spiritual kingdom on earth will we become members of that spiritual kingdom in heaven. Jesus as King now seeks to rule over us. We are not made slaves in His kingdom against our own wills. Instead, we are to become His willing subjects. He becomes truly our personal king when we submit to Him.

# Lesson Eight          Worksheet

*True or False.*

_____ 1. The Bible uses various names when it speaks of the Son of God.

_____ 2. *Jesus* is His personal name which means *Messiah* or *The Anointed One.*

_____ 3. The name Jesus was given to Him before He was born.

_____ 4. Joshua, in the Old Testament, is a type of Christ.

_____ 5. Jesus was the name by which He was known to the disciples.

_____ 6. From His childhood Jesus always thought of the cross as His goal in life.

_____ 7. The Old Testament does not tell us anything about Jesus Christ.

_____ 8. *Christ* is not really a name, but a title which refers to His office.

_____ 9. In the Old Testament, kings received a crown as a sign of their office.

_____ 10. Christ was anointed with oil at the time of His baptism.

_____ 11. The offices of Christ do not tell us much about His life and work.

_____ 12. As a prophet, Jesus Christ came to teach us God's will.

_____ 13. A prophet is one who only predicts future events.

_____ 14. The main work of the Old Testament prophets was to call people to repentance by preaching the Law, and to faith by proclaiming the Gospel.

_____ 15. Unless there is a complete inner change of attitude toward sin and God, we cannot become or remain a member of the kingdom of God.

_____ 16. The prophetic office of Christ ended with His ministry on earth.

_____ 17. A Gospel minister has the highest and most responsible office in the world.

_____ 18. As a priest, Jesus came to atone for our sins and to pray for us.

_____ 19. It was not necessary for Christ to satisfy all the demands of God's Law.

_____ 20. The Law demands that we do only the best that we can.

_____ 21. The Bible tells us that people are good by nature and do not need to be punished.

_____ 22. Jesus became human to fulfill the Law and to bear the penalty we deserve.

_____ 23. The priestly work of Christ involves only His sacrifice for us.

_____ 24. As king, Jesus Christ forces His rule over us.

_____ 25. Only as we by faith in Christ become members of His spiritual kingdom on earth, will we become members of that spiritual kingdom in heaven.

*Completion Questions.*

26. Why was the Son of God given the name *Jesus?*

27. Jesus' official name *Christ* is the _____ form of the Hebrew _____ and means _____.

28. What is the main work of Christ as a prophet?

29. How is the sacrifice of the Old Testament priests different from the sacrifice of Christ?

30. Name and describe each of the three kingdoms over which Christ rules.

   a.

   b.

   c.

*Answer the following questions from your study of Acts 9.*

31. What happened to Saul on the road to Damascus and what was the result?

32. What did the Lord tell Ananias to do to Saul and what was Ananias' reaction?

33. What are the two miracles Peter performed and how did the people respond?

# The Redemption by Christ

## *Assignment*

Read Acts 10. Review the Second Article and its meaning, and study questions 175-183 in the *Explanation of Luther's Small Catechism.* Read this lesson, complete the worksheet and be prepared for a quiz.

*For you know that it was not with perishable things such as silver or gold that you were redeemed from the empty way of life handed down to you from your forefathers, but with the precious blood of Christ, a lamb without blemish or defect. I Peter 1:18-19.*

## The Second Article of the Apostles Creed

"I believe in Jesus Christ, His only Son, our Lord, who was conceived by the Holy Spirit, born of the Virgin Mary, suffered under Pontius Pilate, was crucified, dead, and buried; He descended into hell, the third day He rose again from the dead; He ascended into heaven, and is seated at the right hand of God the father Almighty; from whence He shall come to judge the living and the dead."

The explanation of the Second Article says, "I believe that Jesus Christ...has redeemed me, a lost and condemned creature, bought and freed me from all sins, from death, and from the power of the devil — not with silver and gold, but with His holy and previous blood, and with His innocent sufferings and death — in order that I might be His own, live under Him in His Kingdom, and serve Him..."

## The Meaning of Redemption

The word *redeem* means *to buy back and set free, as a slave.* The dictionary tells us that *redemption* is "the act of obtaining the release or restoration of, as from captivity, by paying a ransom," or "to deliver from sin and its consequences by means of a sacrifice offered for the sinner." When we had shut ourselves out of the Father's house and deserved to be forgotten and left to perish, God provided for our salvation. "For God so loved the world that He gave His one and only Son..." (John 3:16).

## The Need and Purpose of Redemption

The redemption which was first promised in the Garden of Eden, immediately after the Fall, and without which no salvation for us is possible, was accomplished in the fullness of time by Jesus Christ.

The need of redemption is based on the fact that the human race is sinful and that God is righteous. The sinful and lost state in which we find ourselves because of our original and our actual sin is one from which we cannot by any possible means free ourselves. The Bible tells us that we are the servants or the slaves of sin (John 8:34). By yielding to temptation and obeying the devil we cut ourselves off from God and come under the rule of Satan. Sin separates us from our loving Father in heaven and makes us the helpless victims of the enemy. We are neither able nor willing to return. We are lost and condemned. We gave up a blessing and invited a curse. We turned our backs on heaven and were slipping into hell. Our case was hopeless and the end result could only be eternal despair and destruction. If we are to be saved at all, it must be by the grace of God alone. This grace is offered to everyone in Christ the Redeemer, as Paul says, "For the grace of God that brings salvation has appeared to all men" (Titus 2:11).

It is true; God is love and takes no pleasure in punishing sin. Since He is holy and just, He cannot look with favor or indifference on us who are sinful, and whose actions are a constant transgression of His commands. He cannot overlook or excuse sin. While He is a God of love, and wants to save us from our lost condition, He cannot do so in any way which would conflict with His holiness and justice. He would not be God if He stopped being holy and just, just as He would not be God if He stopped being loving and kind. Therefore, when God planned from eternity to save us, His plan of redemption included the satisfaction of His holiness and justice as well as His love.

The purpose of redemption is to restore, or to bring back, the fellowship or communion between us and God which was broken by sin. Jesus said, "I have come that they may have life, and have it to the full" (John 10:10b). Christ has redeemed us "in order that we might be His own." He bought us that we might belong to Him and be free to serve Him in thankfulness and love. No longer under the control of sin or driven by the Law, Jesus leads us to yield ourselves to Him as our Lord. We "live under Him in His kingdom" of grace here on earth and in the heavenly kingdom of glory, and we "serve Him in everlasting righteousness, innocence and blessedness." We serve, not in fear, because we have to, but with a new will, because we want to.

Christ has redeemed us from sin, death and the devil.

1) He redeemed us from the punishment of sin by taking the blame and guilt of our sin upon Himself.

2) He redeemed us from the sting of death by taking away the reason for our fear of natural death and the punishment of eternal death.

3) He redeemed us from the ownership of Satan by freeing us from the power of sin and the control of Satan.

## A Divine Redeemer Is Needed

In order to redeem us, there was needed a person who combined in Himself both a divine and a human nature who was both God and man. Redemption had to come from God in order to be valid for Him, and it had to be carried out in human form in order to be valid for us. Therefore, God from eternity planned to send His only Son into the world. When the right time came, the Son of God became incarnate, that is, was born of a virgin.

## The Price of Redemption

Redemption requires that a ransom must be paid. The Second Article tells us that the price of our redemption was not silver and gold. This was worthless as the price of purchase. This could not buy freedom from spiritual bondage. Nor could the crushing guilt of sin be removed if Christ had been only a great teacher and example.

Our redemption must be with Christ's holy and precious blood. Nothing less could be our ransom. Apart from the shedding of blood there is no forgiveness. Christ shed His blood and gave His life to save us from death. The sinless Lamb of God took upon Himself our sins by offering Himself as a sacrifice in our place. In love He identified Himself with us, took our place and accepted what we deserved in order that by faith we might step into His place and receive what He deserved. The curse we brought upon ourselves fell on Him so that we might inherit an eternal blessing.

This redeeming work of Christ involved unimaginable suffering—spiritually, mentally and physically. It was the inevitable result of His obedience. His death on the cross was the final consequence of that perfect obedience. As the Apostle Paul says, "For just as through the disobedience of the one man the many were made sinners, so also through the obedience of the one man the many will be made righteous" (Romans 5:19). He bore the punishment we deserved and satisfied all the demands of God's justice. He fulfilled the Law. He endured the agonies of hell. He made full and complete atonement for sin. He reconciled us to God. All that He has done for me and in my place is imputed to me by faith in Him as my substitute; that is, it is all counted as if I myself had done it. In this faith I am forgiven and justified in the sight of God and accepted as righteous in His sight.

# The Acceptance of Redemption

The Second Article is the central article of the three articles of the Apostles' Creed. It contains the heart of the Gospel. Christ is the focus of all history, the incarnation of all truth, the sum of all revelation, the Lord of all creation. The crucified and resurrected Jesus Christ was the great theme of the Apostles. This is also the message that brings peace and joy to our hearts.

Even though Christ has paid the redemption price for all people by giving His life a ransom for all, many are eternally lost because they reject Him. Notice how the Article uses the first person singular pronoun, "*My* Lord, who has redeemed *me*...that *I* might be His own." Only as you live in daily repentance and faith in Christ as your Savior from sin, you can say, "This is most certainly true."

A man was found kneeling by a soldier's grave. Someone came to him and said, "Why do you pay so much attention to this grave? Was your son buried here?"

"No," he said. "During the war my family was sick and I was drafted, but I couldn't leave them. One of my neighbors came over and said, 'I will go for you, I have no family.' He went. He was wounded, carried to the hospital and died. That's why I have come many miles to attend to his grave. He died for me!"

Christ was our substitute. He went to fight our battles. He died. He died for you. May God help you to believe in the Lord Jesus Christ as your personal Savior.

# Lesson Nine      Worksheet

*True or False.*

_____ 1. The word *redeem* means to buy back or to set free.

_____ 2. Because God is love, we deserve the salvation He has promised.

_____ 3. The first promise of God's plan of redemption was given to Mary.

_____ 4. Our need of redemption is based on the fact that we are sinful and that God is righteous.

_____ 5. If we try hard enough, we can free ourselves from our lost and sinful state.

_____ 6. The Bible tells us that we are slaves of sin.

_____ 7. Sin separates us from God and makes us the helpless victims of the enemy.

_____ 8. By nature we do not want, nor are we able to, return to God and His grace.

_____ 9. God's grace is offered only to those who will receive it.

_____ 10. God delights in punishing the wicked.

_____ 11. God would not be God if He did not punish sin.

_____ 12. Because God is love and wants to save us, He will at times overlook our lost condition.

_____ 13. Jesus has come to give us a full and happy life.

_____ 14. Jesus frees us from the control of sin and the rule of Satan.

_____ 15. The Christian serves the Lord because he is forced to do so.

_____ 16. The purpose of redemption is to restore the fellowship between us and God which was broken by sin.

_____ 17. Jesus is able to save us only because He was a man.

_____ 18. God planned to send His Son into the world after the fall into sin.

_____ 19. Because redemption is a free act of God's grace, it did not cost Him anything.

_____ 20. There is no forgiveness apart from the shedding of blood.

_____ 21. Christ identified Himself with us and accepted what we deserved so that we might receive what we didn't deserve.

_____ 22. Christ's death on the cross was the final consequence of His perfect obedience.

_____ 23. By faith in Christ I am accepted as righteous in the sight of God.

_____ 24. Christ has redeemed only those who accept Him as their Savior.

_____ 25. Many are eternally lost because they reject Christ.

*Completion Questions.*

26. How does the dictionary define redemption?

27. If we are to be saved, why must it be by God's grace alone?

28. Why cannot God overlook or excuse sin?

29. What is the purpose of God's redemption?

30. What does it mean that God *imputes* righteousness to me by faith?

*Answer the following questions from your study of Acts 10.*

31. Why did God give Peter the vision of the sheet with the unclean animals?

32. In his vision what was Cornelius to do, and why?

33. What was the message Peter brought to the household of Cornelius?

# The Humiliation of Christ

*Assignment*

Read Acts 11 and 12. Review the Second Article and its meaning, and study questions 184-192 in the *Explanation of Luther's Small Catechism*. Read this lesson, complete the worksheet and be prepared for a quiz.

*Christ Jesus...made himself nothing, taking the very nature of a servant, being made in human likeness. And being found in appearance as a man, he humbled himself and became obedient to death—even death on a cross. Philippians 2:5,7-8*

## The Second Article of the Apostles' Creed

"I believe in Jesus Christ, His only Son, our Lord, who was conceived by the Holy Spirit, born of the Virgin Mary, suffered under Pontius Pilate, was crucified, dead, and buried; He descended into hell; the third day He rose again from the dead; He ascended into heaven, and is seated at the right hand of God the Father Almighty; from whence He shall come to judge the living and the dead."

# He Humbled Himself

The Second Article lists the five steps in which Jesus humbled Himself in order to present His salvation to us. To humble oneself means to accept a lowly place, to have a modest sense of one's own significance, or to step down. The five steps of Jesus' humiliation were:

1. *His Conception and His Birth in Poverty.* The Bible tells us that the conception of Jesus in the womb of the Virgin Mary was a miraculous event. Jesus was in every respect like all other children with one exception—He was not begotten of a human father. His Father was God the Holy Spirit. Therefore, Jesus did not possess a nature which would naturally wander away from God into sin. He had the nature of God, and therefore was pure and sinless from the moment of His conception. Jesus Christ did not have a human father. He was conceived in Mary's womb through the power of the Holy Spirit (Luke 1:30-35). God thus was the Father of the human Jesus. Joseph later became the foster father of Jesus when he was married to the Virgin Mary (Matthew 1:20).

The Virgin Mary must have been a godly woman for God to have chosen her to give birth to Jesus. Mary, however, was not sinless. We believe that she, as well as all other people, have sinned and come short of the glory of God (Romans 3:23).

Jesus was born of the Virgin Mary. It was the work of the Holy Spirit that produced from the sinful nature of the Virgin Mary the holy and pure nature of Jesus Christ. Christ's conception was an immaculate conception, that is, pure and undefiled, and only His conception. The Bible tells us that it was a miraculous conception and birth, and therefore we confess that Christ was "conceived by the Holy Spirit, born of the Virgin Mary."

When Jesus was born and became a man, He did not lay aside His deity. He kept all His divine power. This is evident in the revelation of His glory on the Mount of Transfiguration. However, He did lay aside its use and did not exercise it in His own interest. When He became man by "taking the form of a servant," He "emptied Himself" of the right (exclusive privileges) of His Godhead. He was born in poverty. He lived a life of self-sacrifice. He obeyed the Law. He suffered loneliness, misunderstanding, ingratitude, hatred and persecution. He endured the most shameful insults. He was put to death as a criminal. He died a real, physical death, and His corpse was laid away in a grave.

His miracles, His sinless life, and the authority of His teaching reveal glimpses of His divine majesty. Ordinarily He was "found in appearance as a man," accepting the limitations of other men.

2. *His Physical and Mental Suffering.* Throughout His earthly life, Jesus suffered poverty and persecution. His whole life was one of suffering, accepting the consequences of speaking the truth and doing the will of His heavenly Father in a world of falsehood and wickedness. He suffered all the weaknesses, infirmities and temptations known to human beings, and yet He never once fell into sin (Hebrews 4:15 and I Peter 2:21-24).

His greatest suffering was in His contact with sin and in His resistance against the powers of evil in His hours of temptation. This came to a climax at the end of His life when He suffered the agony of Gethsemane in the phony trial before the Jewish council and in His sufferings under

Pontius Pilate, the Roman governor. In the four Gospels we are told of how He was mocked, spit upon, crowned with thorns and beaten. The whole life of Jesus on earth was a life of suffering which was endured for our sakes. Remember, Jesus did not have to endure all of this, but He did it because He loved us and wanted to save us from our sins (Romans 5:8).

3. *His Cruel and Shameful Crucifixion.* Jesus Christ lived a sinless and pure life. Yet in the last hours of His earthly life, He was hung upon a cross to suffer like a criminal. Crucifixion was the common form of execution used in those days to put criminals to death. This method of death was one of the most cruel forms known. People often hung on these crosses for many hours, and sometimes for days before death finally came. Death usually came through starvation, thirst and/or infection.

Jesus was crucified on a Friday at 9 o'clock in the morning. He died at 3 o'clock in the afternoon. The earth was in darkness from twelve to three. Jesus was crucified on a hill called Calvary (known in Aramaic as *Golgotha*, which means "The Place of the Skull") (Mark 15:21-34). Historians tell us that Jesus was first laid on the ground, a bar was put under His outstretched arms, and nails were driven through the right hand and the left hand (or the wrists). He was then hoisted and fastened by means of ropes to an upright post. One nail was driven through each foot or a long spike through both. In the middle of the post was a wooden pin to support the main weight of the body, but this pin also served to keep the body in the same cramped position. Cicero once said that crucifixion should never come to any Roman, much less to him. It came to Jesus who was crucified between two thieves. He became the chief sinner for He bore the sin of us all. We commemorate the anniversary of His death on Good Friday.

4. *His Violent and Lonely Death.* After several hours of suffering upon the cross, the earthly life of Jesus Christ came to an end. The Bible makes it known that His death was real and that He did not merely faint. It should be noted that the life of Jesus was not taken away from Him. Instead He voluntarily gave up His life for us (John 19:30 and I Corinthians 15:3). He suffered and died of His own will. He gave His life voluntarily for our salvation. Jesus told His disciples during His earthly life that He had power to lay down His life, and He had power to receive it again. This was a voluntary act on His part (John 10:17-18). He "became obedient to death—even death on a cross!" (Philippians 2:8). By His perfect obedience, He atoned for our disobedience. His death was *vicarious,* meaning He died as our substitute and in our place.

The saving value and the power of Christ's suffering and death lie in the fact that Jesus was and is God, who according to the human nature suffered and died for us. Jesus Christ died not simply as any other man, but in and with His death He conquered sin, death, hell and eternal damnation. In His death He bore all the penalty for our sins (I John 2:2 and I Peter 2:24). Without this single fact of history, there would be no hope at all for the forgiveness of our sins.

5. *His Burial.* This, too, was a humble ending to a sinless life. The body of Jesus Christ was buried in a borrowed tomb, the tomb of Joseph of Arimathea. Evidently Jesus' family had no place to bury His body.

# What All This Means

Jesus Christ humiliated Himself in this way in order to redeem us (buy us back) to Himself and His fellowship. He became our ransom price. He has done everything possible for us so that we may be saved. He suffered and died for all of our sins. He bore the penalty for every sin of which we may become guilty. He did it by His "innocent suffering and death."

How then may you be saved? There is only one way to be saved and that is to repent of your sin and by faith believe that Jesus' death upon the cross was also for your sin. Jesus invites you to believe this. He is the one who creates faith within you so that you can repent of your sin and believe this wonderful message we call the Gospel.

How can you be sure that you are saved? The Apostle John, referring to Jesus, gave this answer, "Yet to all who received him, to those who believed in his name, he gave the right to become children of God" (John 1:12). In another writing, the Apostle John says, "He who has the Son has life; he who does not have the Son of God does not have life. I write these things to you who believe in the name of the Son of God so that you may know that you have eternal life" (I John 5:12, 13).

# Lesson Ten          **Worksheet**

*True or False.*

_____ 1. Jesus' birth is a part of His humiliation in becoming our Savior.

_____ 2. Humiliation means to step up, to accept a high and noble position.

_____ 3. The *conception* of Jesus was just like any other human being.

_____ 4. Jesus Christ did not have a human father.

_____ 5. God chose Mary to bear the body of His Son and to give birth to that body.

_____ 6. Mary was without sin because she gave birth to the sinless Son of God.

_____ 7. Christ's conception was an *immaculate conception.*

_____ 8. When Jesus was born and became a man, He laid aside His deity.

_____ 9. Jesus laid aside the use of His deity.

_____ 10. Jesus was never misunderstood or insulted during His earthly life.

_____ 11. Jesus was put to death like a criminal.

_____ 12. Because Jesus is God, He did not suffer all the weaknesses, infirmities and temptations known to us.

_____ 13. Jesus' greatest suffering was the physical pain He endured on the cross.

_____ 14. Jesus deserved the suffering He received because He made the people angry.

_____ 15. Jesus Christ lived a sinless and pure life.

_____ 16. Crucifixion was the common form of execution for criminals in those days.

_____ 17. Crucifixion was an instantaneous form of execution.

_____ 18. Jesus was crucified on a hill called *Calvary.*

_____ 19. We commemorate the resurrection of Jesus on Good Friday.

_____ 20. Because Jesus was God, He did not actually die.

_____ 21. Jesus' life was taken away from Him by His enemies.
_____ 22. Without Christ's suffering and death on the cross we would
             have no hope at all for the forgiveness of our sins.
_____ 23. Jesus was buried in a borrowed tomb.
_____ 24. Jesus paid the penalty only for our past sins.
_____ 25. It is not possible for you to know for sure that you are
             saved until after the Day of Judgment.

*Completion Questions.*

26. What are the five steps in Christ's humiliation?

    a.

    b.

    c.

    d.

    e.

27. How was the birth of Jesus not like that of any other child?

28. What do we mean by saying that Jesus death was voluntary?

29. What do we mean by the term *vicarious?*

30. How may you know that you are saved?

*Answer the following questions from your study of Acts 11 and 12.*

31. How did Peter's experience of speaking to the Gentiles
    show that the Gospel of Jesus Christ had also been given to
    them?

32. How was Peter freed from prison?

33. What are your thoughts when your prayers are answered?
    Explain.

# The Exaltation of Christ

*Assignment*

Read Acts 13. Review the Second Article and its meaning, and study questions 193-200 in the *Explanation of Luther's Small Catechism*. Read this lesson, complete the worksheet and be prepared for a quiz.

*Therefore God exalted him to the highest place and gave him the name that is above every name, that at the name of Jesus every knee should bow, in heaven and on earth and under the earth. Philippians 2:9-11*

## The Second Article of the Apostles' Creed

"I believe in Jesus Christ, His only Son, our Lord, who was conceived by the Holy Spirit, born of the Virgin Mary, suffered under Pontius Pilate, was crucified, dead, and buried; He descended into hell; the third day He rose again from the dead; He ascended into heaven, and is seated at the right hand of God the Father Almighty; from whence He shall come to judge the living and the dead."

The explanation to the Second Article says, "I believe...He has done this in order that I might be His own,

93

live under Him in His kingdom, and serve Him in ever-lasting righteousness, innocence, and blessedness; even as He is risen from the dead, and lives and reigns to all eternity. This is most certainly true."

## The Victory of Christ

Just as the Apostles' Creed outlines the five steps in which the Son of God humbled Himself, so it also outlines the five steps in which the Son of God was exalted. To be exalted means to be lifted up in rank, honor, or power, or to receive a high or lofty position.

When Jesus Christ had completed the work of redemption, He again assumed the full use of the glory and power which had belonged to Him as the Son of God. For a time He had laid aside the use of His privileges as God. When His humiliation was complete and the work of redemption was finished, He took back the privileges which belonged to Him at all times as God. His human nature was now to be exalted as he assumed the full use of the power and the glory that was His as God. Jesus had humbled Himself by becoming a human being. Now He was to be exalted as a human being.

## Jesus' Exaltation

The five steps in the exaltation of Christ are:

1. *He Descended into Hell.* The Bible does not tell us much about this first step of victory for Christ. The main Bible passage that supports this statement in the Creed is

found in I Peter 3:18-20. From this passage we learn at least three things:

a. That Christ died for our sins.

b. That He was made alive in the Spirit (that is, He was raised from the dead in a new and spiritual body).

c. That He preached to the spirits who were in prison.

The word *hell* in the Apostles' Creed does not refer to the final place of torment for all lost people. Rather, it refers to a spiritual prison where the souls of the lost people are kept until the day of resurrection. The American Standard Version and the Revised Standard Version of the Bible both use the word *hades* when it has reference to this spiritual prison (Luke 16:22-26 and Revelation 20:14). *Hades* is a place of torment, or a prison for all lost souls. There is no escape from this place. In Hades the lost are simply waiting for the judgment day when they will be brought before the throne of God. There the lost will receive their eternal sentence of being doomed to spend eternity in hell. The word *hell* in the Apostles' Creed refers to this prison for the lost and is called *hades*.

There are four false teachings regarding Christ's descent into hades. They are:

a. That the soul of Jesus went down into *Limbo*, which was the place where the souls of the believers, who had died before Christ, were held.

b. That *hell* was the grave.

c. That He wished to give the damned ones a second chance.

d. That He suffered the torments of hell in His descent.

95

We are not sure just when Jesus descended into hell. It was probably some time early on Easter morning, after He awakened and before He appeared to His disciples, that Jesus descended into hell to show Himself as its conqueror. We, too, as believers, now triumph over Satan and hell through our substitute and champion.

His descent into hell may seem like humiliation, but it was a part of His exaltation because it was the victorious Christ who entered this realm to complete a judgment at the end of one age and the beginning of a new age. He triumphed over the powers of darkness and proclaimed the good news of redemption to those who had waited for Him in faith.

Why did Jesus descend into Hades? The Apostle Peter (I Peter 3:18-20) tells us that He preached to these people. We are not told what He preached. Many believe that Jesus descended into Hades to proclaim His victory over sin, death and the devil. Certainly He did not go there to give them any second chance to be saved. This is not taught any place in the Bible.

2. *The Third Day He Rose Again From The Dead.* The Bible makes it plain that the same Jesus who died on the cross also rose again from the dead (I Corinthians 15:4). The story of His resurrection from the dead is recorded in Matthew 28, Mark 16, Luke 24 and John 20-21. Jesus took again the life He had laid down. The same body that was crucified, dead, and buried was raised alive, transformed and glorified.

The Second Article tells us that on the third day Jesus rose again from the dead. The Jews referred to a part of a day as a day, and so do we. The Article tells us it was on the third day, or the third day after the crucifixion (Good

Friday) that Jesus arose from the dead. This was also the first day of the week (Sunday). It is this event which we celebrate on Easter Sunday.

The death of Jesus had been real, and now His resurrection was also just as real. At first the disciples expressed doubts. However, they were convinced and no longer doubted when Jesus re-appeared to them with the same body which was crucified, the body which bore the marks of the nails in His hands and the spear in His side. At the same time, it was a new body with new properties, transformed and glorified. It was a body that would never die again. In this new body He was able to pass through locked doors. He was able to vanish suddenly from their sight. His body was not hindered by time or space. He passed through the tomb. He arose, leaving the graveclothes undisturbed. The stone was rolled away not to let Christ out but to let the disciples in. He descended into Hades. He appeared to the two on the road to Emmaus. He entered the closed room of the disciples. He ascended into heaven. Yet it was a real body of flesh and bones. His body was different, not like a natural body.

All the details of Christ's resurrection recorded in the Bible prove the reality of His resurrection as a historical fact. His ten appearances to the apostles, to many of the other disciples, and to some of the women believers and the wonderful change that took place in His followers, are evidences that support the resurrection. No other event in history is as widely proven and attested as the resurrection of Jesus Christ.

What are some of these evidences that stand as proof of the resurrection? They are:

a. He predicted it. He Himself spoke of it often. He is the one whose word can be trusted. Not once do we find Him falling short of any of His claims.

b. The empty tomb proved it. The Roman soldiers as well as the disciples saw that the tomb was empty.

c. The many appearances of Jesus to the disciples and others after the crucifixion proves it.

d. Paul's experience and testimony support it.

e. The existence of the church testifies to it.

f. The converting and saving power of the Gospel demonstrates it.

g. The life of countless believers for nineteen hundred years establishes it.

Why was the resurrection of Jesus Christ necessary? Three reasons are:

a. Because Jesus was God, it meant that He must rise again. His being necessitated it.

b. The work He came to do required it. To be our savior, He must be victorious over sin and death.

c. The Christian faith has no validity if the resurrection is not a fact.

The resurrection of Jesus Christ from the dead proves at least three things:

a. That Jesus is who He claimed to be, the Son of God, equal to the Father, and that what He said is the truth. No man can say "Destroy this temple, and in three days I will raise it up," and make his claim good. Only God has power over death. If Christ has power over death, then Christ must be God.

b. That Jesus' mission was fulfilled and that His sacrifice was complete and accepted by the Father.

c. That there will be a resurrection from the dead for all people, both the saved and the lost. If Jesus had not been raised from the dead, then we would have to believe that His claims were false and we could not look forward to our own resurrection. Now that He has been raised, our hearts are assured about His claims for Himself and about our future resurrection.

If people die, shall they live again? In reply Jesus says, "Come to my sepulcher, come see where My body lay. There are the graveclothes, the headdress, the trappings of death, but where am I? I am risen. Why seek the living among the dead? And because I live, you shall live also. I am the resurrection and the life." Yes, we can say with the Apostle Paul in I Corinthians 15:57, "But thanks be to God! He gives us the victory through our Lord Jesus Christ."

3. *He Ascended into Heaven.* Forty days after the resurrection of Jesus Christ from the dead He ascended into heaven (Acts 1:3). For forty days, Jesus made many appearances to His disciples. These were times when He spoke with them, and when He ate food together with them. Only after abundant proof had been given, that He truly was raised from the dead, did Jesus ascend into heaven. His ascension took place in His human nature. It was done visibly before the eyes of His disciples from the Mount of Olives near Jerusalem. The Son of God, having completed the redemption for which He had come to earth, now returned to His heavenly home which has been His from all eternity.

The ascension was Christ's coronation. He came from heaven, and to heaven He would return. He had died once, but He would not die the second time. Instead He visibly ascended on high to prepare a place for His own. His ascension is a pledge of the believer's destiny. All who know and love the Lord Jesus Christ as their Savior will some day also ascend to heaven.

4. *He Is Seated at the Right Hand of God the Father Almighty.* In the Apostle's Creed we speak of Christ now sitting at the right hand of God the Father Almighty. This *sitting* is to be understood in a figurative sense. It means "occupying a position of divine honor and majesty and exercising divine power." Jesus Christ is the supreme Lord to whom all creation must yield obedience and honor (Philippians 2:8-11). The right hand is often an expression used to indicate a position of power and authority.

What is Christ doing in this place of honor? From John 14:1-3 we learn that Jesus has gone to prepare a place for all people who become His children. From Hebrews 7:25 we learn that Jesus prays for us and for the salvation of all people who draw near unto God through Him. From Ephesians 1:20-23 we learn that He occupies a place of authority which is over all earthly authority. From Ephesians 4:10-12 we learn that He has sent forth His servants to proclaim the good news of His coming to earth.

5. *From Whence He Shall Come to Judge the Living and the Dead.* This last step in the exaltation of Christ, His coming again in power and great glory, will be considered in the next lesson.

## Lesson Eleven          Worksheet

*True or False.*

_____ 1. There are seven steps in the exaltation of Christ.

_____ 2. Jesus humbled Himself by becoming a human being.

_____ 3. Jesus was never exalted as a human being.

_____ 4. The first step in the exaltation of Christ is His resurrection from the dead.

_____ 5. *Hades* is a place of torment, a prison for all lost souls.

_____ 6. Jesus descended into hell to give the lost ones a second chance.

_____ 7. Jesus experienced the torments of hell in His descent into this place.

_____ 8. Jesus most likely descended into hell some time early on Easter morning.

_____ 9. It was a humiliating experience for Jesus to descend into hell.

_____ 10. The Bible is not clear on the resurrection of Jesus from the dead.

_____ 11. The same body that was crucified, dead and buried, was resurrected, transformed and glorified.

_____ 12. We celebrate the resurrection of Christ on Good Friday.

_____ 13. The disciples at first doubted that Jesus had risen from the dead but were convinced when He showed them the marks of the nails in His hands.

_____ 14. The resurrected body of Jesus was able to go through closed doors.

_____ 15. Christ's resurrection is one of the best attested events in history.

_____ 16. Jesus Himself never spoke about the resurrection.

_____ 17. The resurrection of Christ is not an important part of our salvation.

_____ 18. The saving power of the Gospel demonstrates the truth of the resurrection.

_____ 19. The resurrection proves that Jesus Christ is God.

_____ 20. If Christ has power over death, then Christ must be God.

_____ 21. The resurrection of Christ has nothing to do with your
future resurrection.

_____ 22. Fifty days after the resurrection Jesus ascended into heaven.

_____ 23. Jesus ascended on high to prepare a place for you.

_____ 24. Jesus is now sitting at the right hand of God because He
has been exalted to a place of power and authority.

_____ 25. The last step in the exaltation of Christ is His coming again.

*Completion Questions.*

26. What are the steps in Christ's exaltation?

a.

b.

c.

d.

e.

27. Why did Jesus descend into hell?

28. Give three evidences for the resurrection.

a.

b.

c.

29. The resurrection of Christ proves what three things?

a.

b.

c.

30. According to Hebrews 7:25, why is Jesus now sitting at the
right hand of God?

*Answer the following questions from your study of Acts 13.*

31. How did the proconsul, Sergius Paulus, come to believe in
Christ?

32. What did Paul tell the people who were gathered in the
synagogue at Antioch?

33. When the Jews refused to listen to Paul and Barnabas, what
did Paul and Barnabas say they were going to do?

102

# The Return of Christ

*Assignment*

Read Acts 14. Review the Second Article and its meaning, and questions 201-205 in the *Explanation of Luther's Small Catechism.* Read this lesson, complete the worksheet and be prepared for a quiz.

*Therefore keep watch, because you do not know on what day your Lord will come. So you also must be ready, because the Son of Man will come at an hour when you do not expect him. Matthew 24:42,44.*

## Jesus Will Come Again

The Bible clearly states that the same Jesus Christ who ascended into heaven will some day come back from heaven to earth. This was the message of the angels to the disciples after Jesus left them to return to His Father in heaven as recorded in Acts 1:11.

Many people may refuse to believe and bow their knees to Christ today, but when He comes again, the Bible tells us that every knee shall bow (Philippians 2:10).

When Jesus returns, however, it will be too late for people to repent of their sins and seek God's forgiveness.

At "the end of this age," Jesus Christ will come again "with power and great glory." He is with us always now, but when He appears visibly it will be to judge the living and the dead. The believers who are then living on the earth, and all who have died in Christ shall come forth to meet Him in the air to be taken to heaven. At the final judgment all the impenitent and disobedient, the unbelievers, shall be brought before Him to hear these awful words, "Depart from me, for I never knew you," and be cast into outer darkness, into the eternal anguish of hell.

From His verdict there shall be no escape, for He is holy and just and His word is final. The Householder shall bind the tares in bundles for the fire (Matthew 13:24-30,36-43), the Fisherman shall cast away that which is bad (Matthew 13:47-50), the Shepherd shall separate the sheep from the goats (Matthew 25:31-46), the Nobleman shall cast out the unprofitable servant into outer darkness (Matthew 25:14-30), and the Judge of all the earth shall do right (Genesis 18:20-33).

## The Order of Events in Christ's Return

The next great event in world history will be the return of Jesus Christ to remove every Christian from the earth. This tremendous event, which we refer to as the rapture of the church, involves the personal return of the Lord Jesus to claim His own. Although the word *rapture* is not found in the English Bible, the thought it expresses is found in the word translated *caught up* in I Thessalonians 4:17. At the same time Jesus will raise from the dead the body of every person who has lived and trusted in Him as

Savior. This we believe on the basis of I Thessalonians 4:13-18. The unsaved will not be raised from the dead at this time. The Bible speaks of two different resurrections; one for the lost and one for the saved—see John 5:28-29 and Revelation 20:6.

After the rapture, when Jesus has come to take His own out of the world to be with Him in heaven, there will be the seven year *Great Tribulation.* This will be a time of persecution such as the world has never known. In Matthew 24:21-22, Jesus spoke of it as follows: "For then there will be great distress, unequaled from the beginning of the world until now--and never to be equaled again. If those days had not been cut short, no one would survive, but for the sake of the elect those days will be shortened." During this time the beast (the Anti-Christ) will rise to power and become the world ruler. The whole world will wonder and be startled. Satan will give him his power and great authority. In this time of one world government, he will require everyone to have the mark of the beast (666) in order to buy and sell. Anyone who refuses will be put to death. He will be the great deceiver.

Toward the end of the Great Tribulation, the armies of the nations of the world will gather in Israel to make war on Jesus Christ. Jesus will then return on a white horse, with the armies of heaven on white horses, and will slay them all with the sword of His mouth. This is called the *Battle of Armageddon* (Revelation 19:11-21). Christ will return to the Mount of Olives to take rulership of the whole earth as King of Kings and Lord of Lords! This is the second part of Christ's return when He shall come to destroy the forces of evil. Then He shall rule the world with His saints for a thousand years. This period of time is called the *Millennium*. During this time Satan will be bound and Christ will rule for a thousand years in peace and righteousness.

Jesus Christ is going to reign over this earth for a period of 1,000 years. It has been almost 6,000 years, according to Bible genealogy, since God created Adam and Eve. They had complete dominion over the earth until they sinned and yielded to the temptation of Satan. Since then Satan has been ruling the earth through the leadership of people. Mankind has failed. Jesus will not fail. His rule will be perfect and just.

After the Millennium, all the lost who have died and yet lived on in Hades will be raised from the dead. These, together with the living unsaved people, will be called before the *Great White Throne Judgment Seat of God*. Here the books will be opened, and anyone whose name is not found written in the book of life will be cast into the lake of fire for all eternity (Revelation 20:15). This horrible future will be faced by anyone who has spurned the love of God and continued in rebellion and unbelief against God. God is a God of love, but He is also a God of wrath. "It is a dreadful thing to fall into the hands of the living God" (Hebrews 10:31).

The last great event is described in II Peter 3:13 and Revelation 21 and 22. Here the Bible speaks of the *new heavens and the new earth*. This is in reality what we mean by *heaven* for the child of God. The Bible does not speak of believers as being bodiless spirits who are to float throughout the universe in the ages to come. Instead it speaks of a new dwelling place which will be just as real as the present dwelling places that Christians now have on earth. It will be a place that will be free from all sin and temptation and where Christians will be free to serve the living God throughout eternity.

## Signs of the Coming of Christ

Jesus told us that we would never know for sure when He would return. As Jesus said, "No one knows about that day or hour, not even the angels in heaven, nor the Son, but only the Father. If he comes suddenly, do not let him find you sleeping" (Mark 13:32,36).

The Second Article does not say when or how Christ will come, but it says He is coming, and why. It simply states the event and the purpose. History tells us of His first coming, and prophecy tells us of His second coming. However, He did give us many signs by which we might know when His return is near. Many of these signs are recorded for us in Matthew 24, Mark 13 and Luke 21. The Apostle Paul also states what world conditions will be like in the end times (II Timothy 3:1-5).

Jesus gives the interpretation of these signs in Luke 21:25-36. Some of the signs given here which shall precede the return of Christ are as follows: there shall be signs in the sun, the moon, and the stars; and on the earth, nations will be in anguish and perplexity; men will faint from terror, apprehensive of what is coming; and the heavenly bodies will be shaken. As we read these signs, and look at the world conditions today, we must earnestly prepare ourselves for the second coming of Jesus Christ, for it may be very near. This great event which we confess in the Apostles' Creed may be much closer to us today than we realize. The second coming of Christ is the Christian's hope and should be our constant inspiration. The assurance that our Lord will come again ought to strengthen us each day and encourage us in our work. His return ought to comfort us in lonely hours and move us to new effort when we are tempted to despair.

## The Events of Christ's Coming

From several passages (See I Thessalonians 4:13-18, I John 3:1-3, I Corinthians 15:51-54, John 14:1-3, Titus 2:11-13, and Philippians 3:20-21), it is evident that the second coming of Christ is an event to which the Christian may look forward to with hope. This event is called "the blessed hope" (Titus 2:13). Certainly for the Christians, it would be a most wonderful event if Christ should return before they must die. The blessed hope is that Jesus may come again before we have to die. Then we would never have to die.

From several other passages (See I Thessalonians 5:1-3, Matthew 25:41,46, II Peter 3:10, Revelation 20:11-15) it is evident that there will be a judgment of the lost when Jesus returns. Christians will not be judged on that day as to whether or not they will be saved or lost. This matter is determined in this present life. When we speak of the Judgment, we speak rather of the final sentence being pronounced before the judgment throne of God upon all who are guilty and lost.

These are the two aspects of Christ's second coming. To the Christians, it will be a time of joy and triumph. To the unsaved, it will be a time of final sentence and departure into the eternal torment of hell.

When Jesus Christ comes again, He will come visibly, suddenly, unexpectedly, with power, and with great glory. Will you be ready for His coming?

# Lesson Twelve        Worksheet

*True or False.*

_____ 1. We cannot be sure that Jesus is coming back to earth again.

_____ 2. When Jesus comes it will be too late for people to repent of their sins and seek God's forgiveness.

_____ 3. All people today believe and willingly bend their knees before Christ.

_____ 4. When Jesus Christ was on earth, He knew the day and the hour when He would return to earth.

_____ 5. When Christ comes again, only the believers will be taken to be with Him.

_____ 6. At the final judgment, all unbelievers will be brought before the Lord.

_____ 7. You can escape judgment if you have lived a good life.

_____ 8. The second coming of Christ should create fear in the heart of a Christian.

_____ 9. There is coming a day of judgment for all unbelievers.

_____ 10. The Christians will also be judged on the day of judgment as to whether or not they will be saved or lost.

_____ 11. The blessed hope of the Christian is that, before he dies, Jesus may come.

_____ 12. It will not be possible for us to know for sure whether we are saved or lost until Jesus comes again.

_____ 13. The next great event in world history will be the *Great Tribulation.*

_____ 14. At the *Rapture* Christ will raise the body of every believer from the dead.

_____ 15. Jesus has foretold that there is coming a time of great persecution.

_____ 16. Satan will give his power and authority to the Anti-Christ.

_____ 17. In the time of one world government, there will be real peace on earth.

_____ 18. During the Tribulation everyone will be required to have the mark of the beast.

_____ 19. Toward the end of the Great Tribulation, Jesus will come from heaven, to slay with the sword of His mouth the nations of the world that come against Israel.

_____ 20. People have ruled over the earth for almost 6,000 years.

_____ 21. Because God is a God of love, He will not send anyone to hell.

_____ 22. Heaven will be a place just as real as our present dwelling place.

_____ 23. A person can know exactly the moment when Christ will come again by observing the signs.

_____ 24. Many of the signs which will precede the return of Christ are present today.

_____ 25. The second coming of Christ is a source of comfort to the Christian.

*Completion Questions.*

26. What message did the angels give the disciples after Jesus ascended to heaven?

27. The return of Jesus Christ to remove every Christian from the earth is referred to as the _____.

28. What is the *Great Tribulation?*

29. What is the *Millennium?*

30. Why is it so important always to be ready for Christ's return?

*Answer the following questions from your study of Acts 14.*

31. What was the reaction of the people when Paul and Barnabas spoke in the synagogue at Iconium?

32. After Paul healed the crippled man at Lystra, who did the people think Paul and Barnabas were?

33. Why did Paul and Barnabas return to Lystra, Iconium and Antioch?

# Unit I Test

## The First and Second Articles

*Assignment*

Review the texts and the worksheets for lessons 1-12 in this book. Review all the memory assignments in the *Explanation of Luther's Small Catechism* for questions 120-205. Know the First and Second Articles, their meanings, and the following questions well: 132, 141, 143, 146, 154, 155, 162, 163, 176, 177, 178, 179, 183, 191 and 205. Review the book of Acts 1-14.

*We are therefore Christ's ambassadors, as though God were making his appeal through us. We implore you on Christ's behalf: Be reconciled to God. God made him who had no sin to be sin for us, so that in him we might become the righteousness of God. II Corinthians 5:20-21*

# Some Facts To Remember

## Introduction

- The purpose of this instruction is to help you to know Jesus Christ as your Savior and to encourage you to be a student of the Word of God.
- The textbooks for this instruction will be the Bible, the *Explanation of Luther's Small Catechism* and this book.

## Lesson 1

- A *creed* is a statement of what a person believes; it is a confession of faith.
- The Apostles' Creed is a brief statement of what the content of the Christian faith is and what every true Christian believes.

## Lesson 2

- The First Article speaks of God the Father and of His work of Creation.
- "I Believe" means I personally know God as my Father and Christ as my Savior. To believe is to *know* with the mind, to give *assent* with the lips, and to *trust* with the heart.
- God is triune. He reveals Himself in three persons: Father, Son and Holy Spirit.

## Lesson 3

- The first person of the Trinity is called the Father because He is the Father of our Lord Jesus Christ and He is the Father of His children in Christ Jesus.

- The fact that God is almighty assures us that He is able to keep you and protect you.
- Angels are actual beings, without bodies, who serve God and God's people.

## Lessons 4 and 5

- God created (brought into being out of nothing) all things in six days by merely speaking a word.
- The angels in heaven and people on earth are the greatest part of God's creation.
- Adam and Eve were made in the image of God, that is, like God in wisdom and holiness.
- Evolution is a theory, not a proven fact, which tries to explain the existence of life.

## Lessons 6 and 7

- The Second Article tells of God the Son and of His work of Redemption.
- It is God's will or purpose that all people should live in fellowship with Him.
- Jesus as man perfectly fulfilled the law and died in our place. As God, His blood had unlimited power to atone for the sins of the whole world.

## Lesson 8

- The personal name of the second person of the Trinity is *Jesus* which means *Savior*.
- The threefold office of Christ is that of Prophet, Priest and King.

## Lesson 9

- Your need of redemption is based on the fact you are sinful and God is righteous.
- The purpose of redemption is to restore, to bring back into fellowship with God.

## Lessons 10 and 11

- Christ humbled Himself by becoming human and dying in your place on the cross.
- Christ was exalted in His victorious resurrection and His glorious ascension.

## Lesson 12

- The Bible tells us that just as Jesus went to heaven, so He is coming back again.
- The order of the final events are: Rapture, Tribulation, Millennium and Great White Throne Judgment.
- No one knows the time of Jesus' return, but the signs indicate it may be soon.

# The Holy Spirit

## Assignment

Read Acts 15. Memorize the Third Article and its meaning, and study questions 206-208 in the *Explanation of Luther's Small Catechism*. Read this lesson, complete the worksheet and be prepared for a quiz.

*But when he, the Spirit of truth, comes, he will guide you into all truth. He will not speak on his own; he will speak only what he hears, and he will tell you what is yet to come. John 16:13*

## The Third Article of the Apostles' Creed

"I believe in the Holy Spirit, the holy Christian church, the communion of saints, the forgiveness of sins, the resurrection of the body, and the life everlasting. Amen."

This article tells us how the Holy Spirit applies the redemption which the Son of God, our Lord and Savior, has accomplished. The Second Article speaks of the work of Christ for us, while the Third Article speaks of the work of the Holy Spirit in us. Both are necessary for our salvation. We are saved by faith in Christ. The Holy Spirit creates this faith and causes us to believe in Jesus unto salvation.

## Review

In the First Article we learned about God the Father and His work of creation. God created the human race and all that exists. People were pure and without sin as they came from the hand of God. Soon they chose to disobey God and walk in their own way. Ever since that time, people have been born into the world as sinful creatures. Now everyone is in need of a Savior to save from a sinful condition and sinful actions.

In the Second Article we learned about Jesus Christ and His work of redemption. Jesus was the Savior which the sinful human race needed. God still loved the human race, even though it had sinned against Him. The love of God was demonstrated in the sending of His Son into the world. Jesus became the Savior of the world by voluntarily laying down His life on the cross. With the death and resurrection of Jesus Christ, it became possible for all people to be saved.

In the Third Article we will learn about the Holy Spirit and His work of *sanctification.* The Holy Ghost and the Holy Spirit are two ways of referring to the same person. The older translations of the Bible used the term Holy Ghost, while the newer translations use the term Holy Spirit. In this and in the following lessons, we shall study the teaching of the Holy Spirit and learn of His person and work.

## The Person and Nature of the Holy Spirit

The Holy Spirit is God (John 4:24). The Holy Spirit is not an *it* or a *thing* or a *force* or an *influence.* The Holy Spirit is a person, the person of God. The term *person* is used in the same sense as in the case of the Father and the Son. The Bible gives to Him divine names, attributes, power, honor and works. We should be careful not to understand or use the word *person* in such a way as to make a separation between the Holy Spirit and the Son and the Father, giving the impression that the one God is three gods. The Holy Spirit is the Spirit of the Father and the Spirit of Christ. The Holy Spirit is the Spirit of the one mind and the one will of God.

In the Old Testament He is presented as the operating presence of God, acting, illuminating, directing, exerting divine power, and therefore *personal.* In the New Testament this truth is made more definite and clear (compare Acts 16:6 with verse 7). All Christians teach that the Holy Spirit is a distinct personality. He is one of the persons of the Triune God, often spoken of as the third person of the Trinity. Some religious groups deny this Biblical teaching about the Holy Spirit.

Matthew 28:18-20 contains the last command Jesus gave to His disciples before He ascended into heaven. He told them that they were to make disciples of all the nations by "baptizing them in the name of the Father and of the Son and of the Holy Spirit." Thus far we have learned that the Father and the Son were distinct personalities. It must follow that the Holy Spirit in this passage is something more than a mere energy or influence. This passage speaks of the Holy Spirit by name, just as it mentions the Father and the Son.

The words in John 14:16-17 were spoken the night before Jesus was crucified on the cross. Here Jesus tells His disciples that He would pray to the Father, that the Father would give them "another Counselor...the Spirit of truth." Note the pronouns which are used in speaking of this Counselor and Spirit: *whom, him, he.* These words speak of a person and not an *it.*

In John 14:26 the Holy Spirit is called a *Counselor.* Note again that the pronouns used here speak of a distinct person: *whom, he.* This verse also speaks of specific actions which the Holy Spirit will take. He will teach us all things and will remind us of everything Christ has said.

In John 15:26 and John 16:7-15 Jesus speaks of the Holy Spirit as a personality who has a work to do.

Acts 2:4 tells of the coming of the Holy Spirit on the day of Pentecost. This was exactly fifty days after the resurrection of Jesus Christ from the dead, and just ten days after His ascension into heaven. On the day of Pentecost the Holy Spirit came to live within the disciples of Jesus. They were "filled with the Holy Spirit." Since then all believers receive the gift of the Holy Spirit when they are saved. Individual believers receive special gifts of the Holy Spirit, which is another subject and will be discussed later.

Other passages tell us that the Holy Spirit inspired and filled Zacharias, Simeon and John the Baptist. By the Holy Spirit, Jesus was born into the world, and by Him He was anointed at His baptism. Works are ascribed to the Holy Spirit that can belong to no one but a person. He is said to come to people, to speak to people, to give gifts to people, to intercede for people, to love people and to be grieved by the actions of people. Divine honor is given to Him. Yes, the Holy Spirit *is* a person.

### Where Does the Holy Spirit Live Today?

In I Corinthians 3:16 and 6:19-20 we find that the Holy Spirit lives in the body of the Christian believer. The Holy Spirit of God does not live in buildings of wood and stone which we sometimes call churches. He lives in the bodies of Christian believers. The body of the Christian becomes the temple or dwelling place of the Holy Spirit.

When we are saved, we may know from what the Bible teaches, that God the Holy Spirit has come to live in our lives. Every Christian has the Holy Spirit in his or her life. If we do not have the Holy Spirit, then we are not

Christians. The Apostle Paul says, "If anyone does not have the Spirit of Christ, he does not belong to Christ (Romans 8:9). Do *you* have the Holy Spirit?

## The Work of the Holy Spirit

Jesus Christ has provided our redemption by His death and resurrection. The work of the Holy Spirit is to reveal this redemption to us. Christ died for all the sins of the world, that is, for all the people of the world. The benefits of this death for sin, however, must be applied individually. This is the work of the Holy Spirit.

Therefore, the work of the Holy Spirit *in* us is as necessary for our salvation as the work of Christ is *for* us. If we are to be saved from our sinful condition and our sinful actions, then we must come to a true and saving faith in Jesus Christ. It is the work of the Holy Spirit to bring us to this true and saving faith.

The work of the Holy Spirit is called *sanctification.* This word is used here in the broad sense of His entire work of "calling, gathering, enlightening, and preserving." It also includes the narrow sense of the work in which the Holy Spirit seeks to daily have the Christian become more and more like Christ.

# Lesson Fourteen        Worksheet

*True or False.*

_____ 1. The Third Article has nothing to do with the work of redemption.

_____ 2. The Second Article speaks of the work of Christ for us, while the Third Article speaks of the work of the Holy Spirit in us.

_____ 3. We are saved by faith in Christ, which the Holy Spirit creates in us.

_____ 4. The First Article tells about God the Father and His work of creation.

_____ 5. Ever since creation, people have been created pure and without sin.

_____ 6. People have always chosen to obey God and to walk in His way.

_____ 7. God has shown His love for us in sending His Son to be our Savior.

_____ 8. The Holy Ghost and the Holy Spirit are two different persons.

_____ 9. The Holy Spirit can best be described as a *force* or an influence.

_____ 10. The Bible gives to the Holy Spirit divine names, attributes and honor.

_____ 11. The Holy Spirit is often referred to as the third person of the Trinity.

_____ 12. The Holy Spirit was not present in the days of the Old Testament.

_____ 13. All religious groups believe in the existence of the Holy Spirit.

_____ 14. John 3:16 contains the last words Jesus spoke to His disciples.

_____ 15. Jesus told His disciples that they were to make disciples of all nations by baptizing them in the name of the Father, Son and Holy Spirit.

_____ 16. Jesus referred to the Holy Spirit as the *Counselor*.

_____ 17. The Holy Spirit is our teacher who makes the works of Jesus known unto us.

_____ 18. The day the Holy Spirit came to dwell within the disciples is Easter Sunday.

_____ 19. We cannot be sure that we receive the gift of the Holy Spirit when we are saved.

_____ 20. The Holy Spirit is said to speak to people, to give gifts to them, to intercede for them and to be grieved by their actions.

_____ 21. The Christian's body is the temple or dwelling place of the Holy Spirit.

_____ 22. The Bible says you are not a Christian if you do not have the Holy Spirit.

_____ 23. Jesus died only for those who would receive Him as Savior.

_____ 24. The Holy Spirit has no part in bringing you to true saving faith.

_____ 25. The work of the Holy Spirit is often referred to as sanctification.

## Completion Questions.

26. In the First Article we learn about _____ and His work of _____. In the Second Article we learn about _____ and His work of _____. In the Third Article we learn about _____ and His work of _____ .

27. How has God demonstrated His love for you?

28. How do you know that the Holy Spirit is a person and not just an influence or spiritual force?

29. Where does the Holy Spirit live today?

30. What is the main work of the Holy Spirit?

## Answer the following questions from your study of Acts 15.

31. Why were Paul and Barnabas received by the apostles and elders, but not by the Pharisees?

32. How did Peter say that the Gentiles, as well as his people, are saved?

33. What caused the separation between Paul and Barnabas?

# The Work of the Holy Spirit

*Assignment*

Read Acts 16. Review the Third Article and its meaning, and study questions 209-216 in the *Explanation of Luther's Small Catechism*. Read this lesson, complete the worksheet and be prepared for a quiz.

*But the Counselor, the Holy Spirit, whom the Father will send in my name, will teach you all things and will remind you of everything I have said to you. John 14:26*

### The Third Article of the Apostles' Creed

"I believe in the Holy Spirit, the holy Christian church, the communion of saints, the forgiveness of sins, the resurrection of the body, and the life everlasting. Amen."

The explanation to the Third Article says, "I believe that I cannot by my own reason or strength believe in Jesus Christ, my Lord, or come to Him, but the Holy Spirit has called me through the Gospel, enlightened me with His gifts, and sanctified and preserved me in the true faith, just as He calls, gathers, enlightens and sanctifies the whole Christian church on earth..."

## Spiritually Helpless

Left to ourselves we would not have, nor could we have, any saving faith. We can no more save ourselves than we could have created ourselves. Our reason is so darkened by sin that we cannot recognize sin as sin, nor see any need of a Savior. In Ephesians 2:1, we read, "As for you, you were dead in our transgressions and sins." Consequently, we have neither the desire nor the ability to believe in Christ. It is necessary, therefore, that the Holy Spirit show us our sinfulness and reveal Christ to us as our only Savior.

In the Third Article we confess in the words of Martin Luther, "I believe that I cannot by my own reason or strength believe in Jesus Christ, my Lord, or come to Him, "for we are by nature:

1. *Spiritually Blind.* By ourselves we cannot see that we are sinful. Neither can we see or understand why an innocent one should suffer and die for us. The Holy Spirit removes the blindness and the darkness from our eyes, and gives us spiritual power to see, understand, and appreciate the gospel, God's plan of salvation. In conversion, we are turned from darkness to light.

2. *Spiritually Dead.* In Ephesians 2:1 we read, "As for you, you were dead in your transgressions and sins." Just as a physically dead person can do nothing to help himself, neither can a spiritually dead person believe. The Holy Spirit comes to give new life and to renew the will. In conversion, we are changed from death to life.

No one is able to believe in Jesus Christ or come to Him through self-effort. However, the Holy Spirit invites all people to believe in Jesus and come to Him. When He convinces a lost sinner to come to Jesus, that lost sinner immediately receives forgiveness as a free gift from God. The Holy Spirit does this by *calling* and *enlightening* through the written and proclaimed Word. By this means He calls all people, and through the same means He creates faith in Jesus as our Savior. Those who accept this offered grace are saved. Those who reject it are lost.

## The Holy Spirit Calls

The Holy Spirit calls us through the Word of God. The Holy Spirit calls people through the Bible as it is read, taught or preached. When the Holy Spirit calls people, He uses the Law and the Gospel. Through the Law He seeks to awaken the conscience of people to see the demands of a holy and a righteous God. He goes on to enlighten them about what will happen if they do not repent and turn in faith to the Savior, the Lord Jesus Christ. When the Law has been allowed to do its work in the conscience of people, the Holy Spirit calls them through the Gospel. It is the Holy Spirit who presents Jesus Christ to them, and calls them to surrender in faith to Jesus. This experience we call *repentance and faith.*

The Holy Spirit calls all people, young and old alike. He calls them through the Means of Grace, the Bible and the Sacraments—that they might repent and believe the gospel of Jesus Christ to the eternal salvation of their souls. The sacraments call people to examine their own hearts and to confess their sins, that they may be assured of God's forgiveness and be strengthened in faith, hope and love.

# The Holy Spirit Awakens and Enlightens

The Holy Spirit first seeks to awaken sinners to their natural sinful condition before God. The Bible tells us that the work of the Holy Spirit is to convince people of their sin. All people are lost in sin, but they may not yet know it. The Holy Spirit uses the Law to awaken sinners to this fact. If you are not saved, the first work the Holy Spirit desires to do in your life is to awaken you to the fact that you are by nature sinful and unclean before a holy God. He wants to bring this matter to your conscience so that you may become alarmed about this condition. When people suddenly become sick, they often become alarmed about what may be the matter. The Holy Spirit wants to alarm you about your sin, so that you will be awakened to the consequences of continuing in this way.

To enlighten means to bring to light and understanding. There are two things which the Holy Spirit desires to show to the awakened sinner. First, He wants to enlighten the sinner about how awful sin actually is. A person may have admitted that he is a sinner, but not until the Holy Spirit has enlightened him has he really seen how awful his sin is in the sight of a holy God. Secondly, the Holy Spirit wants to enlighten the sinner about what Jesus Christ has done for him through His death and resurrection. Jesus will completely pardon, give new life in all its fullness and graciously grant the blessings. As the Holy Spirit awakens and enlightens the sinner about these matters, He then calls him to surrender to Jesus Christ. This is to repent and believe.

# Repentance

When the Holy Spirit is allowed to bring you to repentance, at least four things will happen. The Holy Spirit will lead any sinner who hears the Law and the Gospel, and who does not resist the work of the Holy Spirit. The four experiences in repentance are:

1. *You will admit and confess your sin (Psalm 32:5).* When the Holy Spirit has brought you to an experience of repentance, then you will no longer have any arguments with God about your sin. You will no longer try to defend those things in your life which you know to be wrong. You will admit that God is right about the reality of your sin and you will confess it all to God in prayer.

2. *You will be sorry about your sin (II Corinthians 7:10).* If you are repentant about your sin, you will be truly sorry about the sins which have entered into your life. It will hurt you that you have sinned against God.

3. *You will hate and forsake all sin (Isaiah 55:6-7).* God will give you grace to forsake them. He will enable you to give them up, no matter how much you may have loved them before if you are repentant about your sins.

4. *You will desire to be forgiven (Psalm 51:1-3, 9-10).* Having seen your desperate condition before a holy God, you will earnestly desire to be forgiven.

# Faith

What does God the Holy Spirit do for you when you have allowed Him to enable you to repent? He grants you a true and saving faith in the Lord Jesus Christ. This will be a personal confidence that Jesus Christ has actually saved you and made you a child of God. You will know that all your sins have been forgiven. In true faith you will trust the promises of God's Word.

When we permit the Holy Spirit to bring us to repentance and faith, we are converted and saved. That is, we have turned from sin and self to God and a new life has been born in our hearts. Repentance and faith are continuous experiences in the life of a Christian. We sin daily and therefore we confess our sins to God day by day in true penitence of heart. And day by day we turn to Christ for the assurance of His Word that we are forgiven and saved for His sake. We live in an attitude of repentance and faith.

Salvation is not something that we earn or deserve. Jesus acquired salvation for us and freely gives it to those who will accept it as a free gift of His grace. Nor do we merit anything because of our faith. Faith is merely the empty hand which receives what God offers. Nor are we saved on account of being good or doing good. Good deeds are the fruit of a new life. They are the confession of our faith in Christ and our love for Him. The obedience of faith is the work of the Holy Spirit and His opportunity to transform us into the image of Christ.

Jesus makes it clear that the obedience of love is the required fruit of the Spirit. This love will be evident in a life of doing good, love of other Christians, and love for all people. The conditions of being "preserved in the true faith" are the faithful use of the Word of God, regular communing at the Lord's Table, a life of prayer, careful avoidance of intentional sin, resisting the temptations of the world, the flesh, and the devil, and a glad response to the promptings of the Holy Spirit.

The Christian should avoid whatever may threaten, injure or destroy the life begotten in his heart by the Holy Spirit. In obedience he maintains his union with Christ to exercise and develop the spiritual gifts he has received. He will then grow in grace, serve the Lord in ministering to others, and glorify his Savior in conversation and conduct, testimony and example.

## A Warning

The Bible makes it plain that Christians can fall from grace and be lost. It is possible to grieve the Holy Spirit by continued indifference to His calling and enlightening, until the heart is hardened, and He has to leave them to their fate. Christians may sin against the Holy Spirit, persevering in willful sin, with full knowledge of what is being done, until the unpardonable sin has been committed. The sin against the Holy Spirit is unpardonable, because they deliberately identify themselves with their sin; they dismiss Jesus and quench the Holy Spirit. They then neither desire nor are they able to receive the remission of sins. Those who fear that they may be guilty of this sin have not committed it. Those guilty of it are absolutely indifferent to such a possibility. That is, they do not care. Unless we yield to the pleading of the Spirit of Christ, we are inviting this same result. If we continue in a life of sin, the consequence must be a stifled conscience, a hardened heart, the crossing of the line marked "too late," and a lost soul.

## Summary

In summary, how does the Holy Spirit work in our lives?

1. *He Calls.* When we hear the message of salvation in Christ, realize our sinfulness and need of a sin-bearer, and turn from sin to grace, receiving Christ as our Savior—in that instant we are converted. The Holy Spirit calls by the Gospel.

2. *He Enlightens.* As we continue to read the Bible and pray and fellowship with God's people, our knowledge will grow. More light will be given to our darkened understanding and we will gain a deeper and fuller understanding of God's love for sinful people. In other words, the seed of the Word grows toward the light. This too comes from the Holy Spirit who enlightens us with His gifts.

3. *He Sanctifies.* Soon others will begin to talk about us and say, "Have you noticed the transformation in them. They are changed people. They are so different from the way they used to be. They are honest, kind, forgiving, caring, pleasant and zealous unto every good work." What took place? The plant has brought forth fruit. The Holy Spirit sanctifies, renews the will and leads to do the good and shun the evil.

4. *He Keeps.* Only through the grace of God and the work of the Holy Spirit can we be kept in true faith to the end.

Therefore, from beginning to end, salvation is because of the work of the Spirit of God. We cannot contribute one thing towards our salvation. However, we can say, "Praise, honor, and glory be to God." May this be true in our lives.

# Lesson Fifteen          Worksheet

*True or False.*

_____ 1. Left to ourselves we would not have and could not have any saving faith.

_____ 2. We are able to recognize sin and our need of a Savior by our reason.

_____ 3. The Bible tells us our natural desire is to believe in Christ.

_____ 4. The Holy Spirit is not needed to show us our sinfulness.

_____ 5. In the Third Article we confess we cannot come to Jesus by our own strength.

_____ 6. The Bible tells us that by nature we are spiritually dead.

_____ 7. The Holy Spirit calls only those who will believe.

_____ 8. The Holy Spirit calls us through the Bible.

_____ 9. Through the Law, the Holy Spirit awakens us to see the demands of a holy and righteous God.

_____ 10. The Holy Spirit calls us through the Gospel, which tells us what we should do and what we should not do in order to be saved.

_____ 11. The Holy Spirit calls us to repent and believe the Gospel.

_____ 12. All the people of the world know that they are lost in sin.

_____ 13. The Holy Spirit comforts us by not troubling us about our sin.

_____ 14. To enlighten means to bring to light and understanding.

_____ 15. We can be repentant even if we resist the work of the Holy Spirit.

_____ 16. The first step in repentance is to admit that we have sinned and confess it to God.

_____ 17. As long as we are sorry for our sin, we do not have to forsake it or give it up.

_____ 18. When we permit the Holy Spirit to bring us to repentance and faith, we are converted and saved.

_____ 19. Repentance and faith are continuous experiences in the Christian life.

_____ 20. Salvation is something we can earn and deserve by being good or doing good.

_____ 21. Bible reading, prayer and Christian fellowship, are not necessary for being preserved (or kept) in the true faith.

_____ 22. The Christian should be careful to avoid whatever may threaten spiritual life.

_____ 23. A Christian is in no danger of falling from grace and being lost.

_____ 24. When we become Christians, it will be evident in our outward lives.

_____ 25. From beginning to end, salvation is the work of the Holy Spirit.

*Completion Questions.*

26. What are the Means of Grace?

27. What two main things does the Holy Spirit enlighten us to see?

    a.

    b.

28. What are the four experiences in repentance?

    a.

    b.

    c.

    d.

29. Why must repentance and faith be a daily experience?

30. What are the four main aspects of the Holy Spirit's work?

    a.

    b.

    c.

    d.

*Answer the following questions from your study of Acts 16.*

31. What vision did Paul have when he was in Troas and why was it given to him?

32. Why was Lydia ready to hear the gospel?

33. Why was the Philippian jailor frightened by the earthquake and what did he do when it came?

# Faith and Justification

*Assignment*

Read Acts 17. Review the Third Article and its meaning, and study questions 217-224 in the *Explanation of Luther's Small Catechism*. Read this lesson, complete the worksheet and be prepared for a quiz.

*For all have sinned and fall short of the glory of God, and are justified freely by his grace through the redemption that came by Christ Jesus....For we maintain that a man is justified by faith apart from observing the law. Romans 3:23,24,28*

## What Happened?

What happens to us when the Holy Spirit has been allowed to bring us to repentance over our sin and faith in the Lord Jesus Christ? What has God done for us in that moment? Several words are often used to describe what God has done. Some of these words are: justification, regeneration or the new birth, conversion and salvation.

When we use these words we are not speaking of something which we must do ourselves in order to be saved. Instead, we are speaking of something which the Holy Spirit must do in us. When we have been brought through the experience of repentance and faith, then it may be said that we have been justified, regenerated, converted and saved.

## Faith

Believing in Christ is essential if we are to be saved. This believing is the work of the Holy Spirit in us. By His holy life and innocent death, Christ has acquired merit and righteousness for all. All that God asks of us is that we believe in Christ as our Savior so that His merit and righteousness may be counted as ours. Salvation is through faith alone. It is, therefore, very important that we know what is meant by saving faith.

## Saving Faith

The Bible tells us that faith is trust in God as the God of salvation. Faith is a conviction of things not seen, a certainty concerning invisible realities (Hebrews 11:1). Faith is confidence in spite of appearances to the contrary (Romans 4:18). Faith is seeing in Christ the absolute revelation of God (John 14:9).

Much that is called faith today is not faith in the sense in which the Bible uses the word. Saving faith is not just a belief that the gospel is true, nor is it just an intellectual acceptance of certain doctrines about Christ. It is something much more fundamental. Saving faith may be defined as an entirely new attitude toward Christ the Savior, or the promise of salvation, which God has given to us in Christ.

## Faith and Justification

From these definitions we see that the essential thing about faith is confidence—confidence in Christ or the promise of God given to us in Christ. As was outlined in Lesson Two, faith has been described from three different viewpoints, namely: knowledge, assent, confidence or trust. We must know about the grace of God in Christ. We must give assent to God's promise. And we must have confidence in it. The Apostle Paul said, "How, then, can they call on the one they have not believed in? And how can they believe in the one of whom they have not heard" (Romans 10:14). Saving faith has been illustrated by Erwin Kurth in this way, "I know the history of Christ's life and death. I assent to it as historically true. (Historic faith; the devils have historic faith.) Saving faith goes one step farther. I rely upon the result of that history for my salvation." *(Catechetical Helps,* Concordia Publishing House, page 68.) In the end faith is confidence or trust.

## Knowledge

Knowledge as an aspect of saving faith is not simply an intellectual or historical acquaintance with the facts and truths of the gospel. Rather, knowledge is the inner spiritual understanding of God's grace in Christ which comes from the illumination of the Holy Spirit through the Word. Unless this inner knowledge is produced in us, there can be no saving faith (I Corinthians 2:14).

## Assent

Assent as an aspect of saving faith is not simply an intellectual agreement with the truth of the gospel, such as we can give by our own powers. Rather, it is that certain conviction of the heart concerning the truth of the gospel and its significance for my own soul, which is produced by the Holy Spirit. If assent does not go beyond intellectual agreement, it is mere belief, or historical faith, not saving faith.

## Confidence

Confidence is the act of the will by which we confidently rely on Christ as Savior. Faith means trusting in or having confidence in Christ as Savior. It is relying on Him as the foundation of our salvation. When we have this faith, this trust or confidence, we can say, "Christ gave Himself for me. I am saved in Him."

## The Cause of Faith

The Holy Spirit produces saving faith in our hearts. Because of original sin we are not only born without trust or confidence in God, but we cannot by our own powers understand or receive saving faith. The faith which we need for salvation must be produced in us by the work of the Holy Spirit through the Word. This the Holy Spirit does as He convicts us of our sin, leads us to repentance as we feel the pain and misery of living in sin, and reveals Christ to us as our only salvation.

## The Value of Faith

The saving power of faith lies not in the faith itself but in that which it depends and relies on, namely Christ and His merits. The beggar who sits on the sidewalk and holds out his hand for money receives money, not as a reward for holding out his hand, but as an act of grace and pity on the part of the passerby. The empty hand has no financial value in itself; it has value only when it grasps the gift. The value lies in the gift, not in the hand. However, the hand is the instrument through which the gift becomes his. Faith is not a merit which causes God to forgive us and reward us with salvation. The saving power of faith lies altogether in the merit and righteousness of Christ. It is not the faith itself, but the object of faith that saves. The basis of our salvation is the work of Christ. Faith is simply the means through which salvation is accepted.

## The Twofold Effect of Faith

The twofold effect of faith is justification and sanctification. Through faith we are justified before God and through faith we also become sanctified in heart and life. Justification and sanctification must not be confused. Sanctification will be discussed in a later lesson.

## Justification

The immediate result of faith is justification. Justification means that we are forgiven and that the perfect righteousness of Christ is imputed to us (accounted by God to us, or counted as belonging to us) who trust in Him alone for life and salvation. Our state is that of sinners, but our standing is that of forgiven sinners and accepted children of God.

Justification does not refer to any moral quality in us and it does not produce any inner change in us. It is the establishment of a new relationship between us and God. When we deserve only wrath and condemnation, God regards us in Christ as having paid the full penalty of not keeping the law. He treats us as if we had never sinned at all.

We are justified by or through faith. This does not mean that we have been made personally righteous or holy, but that we have been pronounced or declared righteous for Christ's sake. The word *justification* is used in a court of law. That is the sense in which the word is used here. It means a judicial act of acquittal. It is the judgment of God upon us with respect to the divine law. It means that we are pronounced *not guilty* but *righteous* for Christ's sake. It is not something which takes place within us. It is an *external* judicial act of God.

Justification is that act of God by which, for the sake of the obedience of Christ in our place, He graciously and freely forgives the sinner who believes in Christ as Savior and regards him as a righteous person. When God looks upon us in Christ, He no longer sees our sin and unrighteousness, but He sees the righteousness of Christ. The only way we can possibly stand before God is by the imputation of the perfect righteousness which Christ has acquired for us.

# Lesson Sixteen        Worksheet

*True or False.*

_____ 1. When we have been brought through the experience of repentance and faith, then it may be said that we have been saved.

_____ 2. Justification is something we must do ourselves in order to be saved.

_____ 3. It is the work of the Holy Spirit to produce faith in our hearts.

_____ 4. Our salvation is through faith and by doing the best that we can.

_____ 5. Christ's holy life and innocent death provide righteousness for all.

_____ 6. Obedience is not a necessary part of saving faith.

_____ 7. People always speak of faith in the sense in which the Bible uses the word.

_____ 8. Faith is confidence in spite of appearances to the contrary.

_____ 9. The most important element in saving faith is knowledge.

_____ 10. Faith unites us in personal fellowship with Christ.

_____ 11. Saving faith is looked upon as merely knowledge and assent.

_____ 12. Knowledge as an aspect of saving faith is only an intellectual acquaintance with the gospel.

_____ 13. Assent is the conviction of the heart concerning the truth of the gospel for my own soul.

_____ 14. Confidence is relying on Christ as the foundation of our salvation.

_____ 15. Confidence is merely a good feeling, or a sense of certainty.

_____ 16. By nature we desire to put our faith in God.

_____ 17. The faith we need for salvation is produced by our own understanding.

_____ 18. The Holy Spirit convicts us of our sin and reveals Christ to us as our only salvation.

_____ 19. The saving power of faith lies in the faith itself.

_____ 20. Faith is simply the means through which salvation is accepted.

_____ 21. The immediate result of faith is justification.

_____ 22. Justification means that we are forgiven and that the perfect righteousness of Christ is counted as belonging to us.

_____ 23. Justification is a legal word which means a judicial act of acquittal.

_____ 24. When God looks upon us in Christ, He no longer sees our sin and guilt but the righteousness of Christ.

_____ 25. Justification produces an inner change within our heart.

*Completion Questions.*

26. Give three words which are commonly used to describe what God has done for us.

    a.

    b.

    c.

27. What is the difference between intellectual faith and saving faith?

28. What are the three aspects of saving faith?

    a.

    b.

    c.

29. What gives faith its saving power?

30. What is meant by justification?

*Answer the following questions from your study of Acts 17.*

31. What did the Christians in Berea do that caused them to have a more noble character than those in Thessalonica?

32. Why was Paul distressed when he came to Athens?

33. What did Paul say to the people when he saw the altar with the inscription "To an unknown god"?

# Regeneration and the New Birth

*Assignment*

Read Acts 18. Review the Third Article and its meaning, and study questions 225-231 in the *Explanation of Luther's Small Catechism*. Read this lesson, complete the worksheet and be prepared for a quiz.

*In reply Jesus declared, "I tell you the truth, no one can see the kingdom of God unless he is born again. . . . Flesh gives birth to flesh, but the Spirit gives birth to spirit. You should not be surprised at my saying, 'You must be born again.'" John 3:3,6-7*

## The Third Article of the Apostles' Creed

"I believe in the Holy Spirit, the holy Christian church, the communion of saints, the forgiveness of sins, the resurrection of the body, and the life everlasting. Amen."

In the preceding lesson, several different words were given to describe what God does when the Holy Spirit has been allowed to bring us to repentance and faith. They were justification, regeneration or the new birth, conversion, and salvation. Lesson Sixteen was on justification. This lesson will deal with the remaining words. Although these words are quite similar, there are certain distinct differences.

## Regeneration

To regenerate means "to cause to be reborn spiritually." When the Holy Spirit brings a lost sinner to repentance and faith, at that moment the lost sinner is born anew and God immediately gives new life. Jesus said to Nicodemus in John 3:3, "Unless a man is born again, he cannot see the kingdom of God." This is what we mean when we speak of the new birth. All people must be born again (that is, born from above, born anew, regenerated) if they are to enter and see the kingdom of God.

Regeneration may be defined as the act of God by which He gives to the repentant sinner new spiritual life. Regeneration, then, refers to the creation of a new spiritual life that is brought about through faith in Christ. It takes place at the same time as conversion. It deals with that inner change from a state of unrepentance and unbelief to one of repentance and faith. Regeneration means that God makes the sinner a believer, and thus gives a new spiritual life. Justification (from Lesson Sixteen) means that God considers the believing sinner righteous for Christ's sake.

An important part of this new life is faith. Wherever faith is present, there the new life is also present. Wherever faith is lacking, the new life also is lacking. Since we do not really know what life is, even though we can see evidences of life, it is best to define regeneration by giving characteristics of a regenerate person.

A regenerate person is one who has been brought by the Holy Spirit to faith in Christ, and thus has been born again as a child of God. A regenerate person is a believer, and a believer is a regenerate person. Therefore, we can say that regeneration is the act by which the Holy Spirit makes one a believer. A state of faith is a state of regeneration.

## A New Kind of Person

In regeneration, as in conversion and repentance or change of mind, we become new persons, we are born again. This does not mean that we are in any way changed in substance as a person, but that we have been made over with respect to our spiritual life. That which before was dead has been made alive. We become new persons in the sense that our attitudes, our thinking and our ambitions have been changed.

Faith is the beginning of a new life in Christ. When we have faith, we are made spiritually alive. We are inwardly transformed by God's grace. We become a child of God by faith in Christ Jesus (Galatians 3:26). We are brought out of darkness into the kingdom of God's dear Son (Colossians 1:13). We are children of God instead of children of sin. We receive a new birth and become new persons, new creations (II Corinthians 5:17). We will live new lives (Romans 6:4). And we will serve in the new way of the Spirit (Romans 7:6). By nature we are in a condition of spiritual death, dead in transgressions and sin. By being brought to faith we have been made alive.

## Regeneration Is God's Gift to Us

Regeneration is entirely the work of God and not at all our work. The Bible says that by nature we were "dead in transgressions and sins" (Ephesians 2:1). No dead person can make himself or herself alive. Likewise, spiritually dead people cannot possibly give life to themselves. They can be made alive by the Holy Spirit through the Word. They become new persons when they are regenerated, born anew. Literally, they become "children of God" (John 1:12).

Regeneration is God's gift to us. We cannot cause ourselves to be born anew. However, we can receive this gift of life from God. We receive it by the Holy Spirit working true repentance and faith in our souls.

We must remember that we are here speaking of regeneration through the Word, and in that sense it is identical with conversion. The Holy Spirit works in our hearts through the Word until we come to faith, and thus become spiritually alive. We then understand the spiritual significance of the Gospel, recognize the sinfulness of sin, grieve over its guilt and power, appreciate the grace of God in Christ, and trust in Him as our Savior for forgiveness and salvation. The outward evidence that we are spiritually alive is seen in the fact that our faith at once begins to produce love and good works.

## Conversion

To convert means to "turn from one belief or course to another." When the Holy Spirit has brought a person through the experience of regeneration, and has justified that person, then it may be said that the Holy Spirit has brought about a conversion. The Holy Spirit has turned this one away from sin to the Lord. Before conversion, this person was by nature on the road leading to hell. After conversion, this one has been given a new nature and is on the way to heaven.

## A Crisis-Experience

From earliest childhood many have believed what they were told about the gospel of Jesus Christ. They have never disbelieved God. Yet, they may not have the assurance of salvation. If they were asked about their relationship to Jesus Christ, they would not know. This is because they have not entered a conscious fellowship with God. There must come a time when infant faith, which was received in baptism as a gift from God, becomes conscious faith. This is often referred to as a crisis-experience. This experience is characterized by a realization of one's own sinfulness, a conscious acceptance of the grace of God, and the surrender of one's life to Christ. Everyone must come to rely only on the grace of God for salvation. C. Christiansen, in *A Biblical View of the Sacraments*, says "A person must constantly be on the alert against the danger of considering himself a Christian because he has been baptized as an infant, has godly parents, is living a good life, and is faithful in church attendance, etc. When these are relied on for salvation they become pitfalls of self-righteousness into which so many have fallen." (Faith and Fellowship Press, Fergus Falls, Minnesota.)

Others may have believed as little children, but as they grew older they chose a life of sin and rebellion against God. Some may have never believed even as little children. They do not know what it is to live in fellowship with God. All need to be converted from a life in sin to the life in Christ. The work of the Holy Spirit is to convict them of their sin and to lead them to trust in Jesus as their personal Savior. The assurance of salvation comes only through repentance and faith in the Lord Jesus Christ, as promised in the Word of God (I John 1:9, John 1:12, Ephesians 2:8-9).

## Salvation

This is the free gift of God. It belongs to all God's children. Thus far, we have studied the way in which the Holy Spirit works to bring this gift to us. Through the Law, He convicts us of our sin, thus seeking to lead us to true repentance. Through the Gospel, the Holy Spirit shows us the way of salvation through Jesus Christ. When He has brought us to faith in Jesus Christ as Savior, then He at the same time regenerates us and causes us to be born anew as God's children. As God's children, He justifies us from all guilt. Thus He has converted us.

## By Faith Alone

The Bible declares many times that faith will never be ours by working for it or trying to do the best we can. Instead, it declares clearly and emphatically that faith comes as a gift to us from Jesus Christ. Salvation is received only through faith in the Lord Jesus Christ.

# Lesson Seventeen        Worksheet

*True or False.*

_____ 1. The Third Article is about Christ's work of redemption.

_____ 2. It is the Holy Spirit who brings us to repentance and faith.

_____ 3. Jesus said to Nicodemus in Matthew 3, "You must be born again. "

_____ 4. The new birth refers to the new body we receive when we enter heaven.

_____ 5. All people must be born again if they are to enter the kingdom of God.

_____ 6. Regeneration refers to an act of God which takes place for us in heaven.

_____ 7. Justification means that God counts the believing sinner as righteous.

_____ 8. Where faith is lacking, there the new life is also lacking.

_____ 9. A regenerate person is one who has been brought by the Holy Spirit to true faith in Christ.

_____ 10. It is not always necessary to be born again to be a Christian.

_____ 11. Regeneration is something we must work for to receive.

_____ 12. To become a Christian is to allow the Holy Spirit to do His work in the heart, so that Jesus Christ can come in with His life.

_____ 13. In regeneration we become a new person, that is, we are born again.

_____ 14. The new birth has nothing to do with our attitudes or our thinking.

_____ 15. Faith is the beginning of a new life in Christ.

_____ 16. By nature we are spiritually alive and do not need the new birth.

_____ 17. In conversion, the Holy Spirit turns a person away from sin and to the Lord.

_____ 18. Before conversion, a person is on the way that leads to hell.

_____ 19. There must come a time when infant faith becomes conscious faith.

_____ 20. The assurance of salvation is based on our feelings.

_____ 21. It really does not matter what we believe as long as we sincerely believe something.

_____ 22. It is impossible to fall away from Christ once we accept Him as Savior.

_____ 23. Everyone must be converted to enter heaven.

_____ 24. We must live a good life in order to receive God's plan of salvation.

_____ 25. The Bible tells us many times that we will never be saved by our own good works or by trying to do the best we can.

*Completion Questions.*

26. Define regeneration.

27. How do regeneration and justification differ?

28. In what ways do we become new persons when we are born again?

29. Why do many who believe not have the assurance of salvation?

30. How does the Holy Spirit work to bring us to salvation?

*Answer the following questions from your study of Acts 18.*

31. What did the Lord say to Paul one night in a vision?

32. What false charge did the Jews bring against Paul?

33. Who did Priscilla and Aquila meet in the synagogue, and how did they help him?

# Sanctification and Spiritual Growth

## Assignment

Read Acts 19. Review the Third Article and its meaning and study questions 232-236 in the *Explanation of Luther's Small Catechism.* Read this lesson, complete the worksheet and be prepared for a quiz.

*You were taught, with regard to your former way of life, to put off your old self, which is being corrupted by its deceitful desires; to be made new in the attitude of your minds; and to put on the new self, created to be like God in true righteousness and holiness. Ephesians 4:22-24*

## Sanctification

Sanctification is the chief work of the Holy Spirit. In an earlier lesson we stated that the chief work of God the Father was creation, and the chief work of God the Son was redemption.

The first work of the Holy Spirit is to make Christians out of lost sinners. This is sanctification in the broad sense of the term. A Christian is a person who has been "set apart" for Christ and His service. In the broad sense, then, to be sanctified is to be saved. It is to become a Christian. The second work of the Holy Spirit is to enable Christians to live Christ-like lives. This is sanctification in the narrow sense of the term. Sanctification in this sense began in my life the moment I was saved by the Holy Spirit of God. Here sanctification is a process, an ongoing experience throughout the rest of the Christian's life upon earth.

Sanctification is the continuous process through which the Holy Spirit makes believers holy in heart and life. He cleanses them from sin, fills their hearts with love to God and neighbor, gives them power to walk in newness of life and makes them Christ-like and heavenly-minded. As Professor Joseph Stump said, "Faith in Christ does not at once make us perfectly holy and sinless, as some persons maintain; but it takes away the guilt of our sin. We are completely justified and forgiven as soon as we believe; but we are not completely sanctified. Sanctification is a gradual process which will be completed only when we are transformed and glorified in heaven." (*A Study Course in Luther's Small Catechism* by C. J. Sodergren, Augsburg Publishing House, Page 73.)

To sanctify means "to set apart, to hallow." This is what the Holy Spirit seeks to do for us and in us. He first seeks to set us apart from those people who are lost. He sets us apart when He is allowed to work salvation in our hearts. After having set us apart in salvation, He begins immediately to hallow (make holy) our lives. When we believe, we are immediately made holy in the eyes of God, but this holiness is then to be lived out in our day to day living.

## Birth First

Before we can begin to grow and become better Christians we must first become Christians. Before we can experience sanctification (in the narrow sense) in our lives, we must experience salvation. A baby must be born first before it can begin to grow and mature as an independent individual.

## Growth Second

After we are saved, we are commanded by God to continue on and grow. The Apostle Peter writes, "But grow in the grace and knowledge of our Lord and Savior Jesus Christ" (II Peter 3:18). To grow in grace is to love Jesus Christ more and more as we continue to see how much He has done for us in saving us. To grow in knowledge is to learn more and more about Jesus Christ. We are commanded in the Bible to grow in grace and knowledge.

## How Do We Grow?

Our human bodies grow, develop and mature as we eat, breathe, rest and exercise. We will grow spiritually much in the same manner. The following are some of the ways:

1. *Read your Bible every day.* This is where God talks to you. Jesus once said, "It is written: 'Man does not live on bread alone, but on every word that comes from the mouth of God'" (Matthew 4:4).

A good place to start reading your Bible is in the New Testament books, together with the Old Testament book of Psalms. Read one of the Gospels first. Do not attempt to read long portions first. Read slowly and thoughtfully a full paragraph or a short chapter. Then stop to think about what God has said to you. If you find that He is talking to you about a particular thing in your life, be sure to obey the Lord.

2. *Pray every day.* In prayer we talk to God. Prayer to the soul is like air to the lungs of the body. Without prayer, our spiritual lives soon become dead and cold. For real spiritual health, there must be good breathing in the Christian life. A good time to pray is right after you have read a passage from the Bible. Then you can go to the Lord in prayer and talk to Him about what you have read. This is the time to name your sins to God of which you feel guilty. It is a time to ask for His forgiveness and at the same time to thank Him for His forgiveness. In prayer we can also talk to God about our unsaved friends, that they too may be saved. Here we can ask God for specific help to overcome temptation and sin and to help us serve other people.

3. *Attend worship services regularly.* This becomes another way of both "eating" spiritual food and "breathing" in prayer to God. It also provides you with fellowship with other Christians. Jesus said, "For where two or three come together in my name, there am I with them" (Matthew 18:20). When you worship with others you have the promise of Jesus that He also is there with you.

4. *Read good Christian literature.* Search for magazines and books which are distinctly Christian. Here you will find help for living the Christian life.

5. *Tell someone else about Jesus.* Witnessing to others is a form of spiritual exercise. This does not mean arguing religion. To tell someone else about Jesus is to witness

about what Jesus means to you and what He has done for you. If you are saved, you should pray that the Lord will use you to win someone else for Him.

Another way to witness is by caring for people and their physical needs. Help those who are hurting, visit those who are sick, feed those who are hungry and talk to those who are lonely.

## A Life of Service

In Romans 12:1-2, we find an appeal given to the Christian believers to offer their bodies as "living sacrifices" to God. The Holy Spirit wants to do a work in your life. He calls you to present your body in surrender to Him and His power. At the same time He says "Do not conform any longer to the pattern of this world, but be transformed." God does not want your life and actions to be like those of the unsaved. Instead He wants your life to be transformed into a life of service like that of the Lord Jesus Christ.

## A Life of Choosing

In Romans 6:12-14 and 6:16 we find that choices are constantly placed before us. Even after you become a Christian, the devil still wants sin to rule in your body and life. However, if Jesus Christ now dwells in your life, sin must no longer be allowed to reign. A choice is placed before you. With every temptation coming your way, you are to turn to God for deliverance.

# The Two Natures in You

Young people and adults are often confused at what they find within themselves. They have somehow thought that when they become Christians they would no longer face temptations. Often they have thought that they would no longer have desires to sin against God. Here we must remember that within the Christian believer there live two natures.

*The Old Nature* - This is the nature with which we were born. We have noted that its natural desire is to drift or run away from God. This old nature does not change. It remains sinful and evil. Through this old nature the devil constantly comes to tempt us to sin.

*The New Nature* - This is the gift which the Holy Spirit gives to us when we are made Christians. This new nature is the Holy Spirit Himself who now comes to dwell in the believer's life. He does not want the believer to sin against the Lord.

*The Struggle* - The Apostle Paul speaks of the struggle he had with the two natures in Romans 7:14-25. He also writes of this conflict between the two natures in Galatians 5:16-18, "So I say, live by the Spirit, and you will not gratify the desires of the sinful nature. For the sinful nature desires what is contrary to the Spirit, and the Spirit what is contrary to the sinful natures. They are in conflict with each other, so that you do not do what you want. But if you are led by the Spirit, you are not under law."

With each temptation comes a choice. You have no power of your own to fight against the temptations of the devil, but the Holy Spirit within you will give you power to resist as you turn to Him. The Christian life was begun in faith, and it must be continued in faith.

# Specific Sins To Be Avoided

In Galatians 5:16-23 and in Colossians 3:5-17, we find a number of sins which should not be part of the life of the Christian believer. In these Bible passages we see many of the ways by which the devil will appeal to our old nature. As he does this, he seeks to make us fall into sin. The Christian is, however, to be on guard against these suggestions from the devil. When the Christian senses the temptations of the devil to sin in these ways, he or she should turn quickly to Jesus Christ in faith, seeking strength to win the battle within.

*Thoughts* - All of the sins mentioned in these passages really begin with our thoughts. It is here that the battle must be won if these thoughts are not to result in sinful actions. We find that the Bible speaks much about the sins which have a direct effect upon our bodies. Here there is a clear call to pure living. Pure lives, however, come only as there is pure thinking. Our thoughts will be built much upon what we read, hear or see. This is why it is so important that the Christian not neglect to read the Bible regularly. If our minds become full of God's Word, then it will become much more difficult for the devil to penetrate into our thought life with his suggestions of sin against God.

*Words* - These are the products of our thoughts. In these Bible verses from Galatians and Colossians we find a call to purity and truthfulness.

*Deeds* - Deeds are also products of our thoughts. The things which we think about doing we will often do.

*When To Win The Battle* - The battle over specific sins in our lives should be won the moment the devil suggests them to our minds. Whenever there is a temptation to go against what God has revealed to us in the Bible, we should immediately turn anew to the Holy Spirit's power, so that He might grant to us the power of resistance against sin.

Christians are people who love the Lord and no longer want to sin against the God they love. However, they are faced with many temptations, and at times the devil may win a victory by causing them to sin. What should they do when they sin after they have been saved?

When we sin we should immediately return to Jesus Christ to confess our sin and seek His forgiveness. As the Bible says, "If we confess our sin, He will forgive our sin and cleanse us from all unrighteousness" (I John 1:9). In this way we will be kept in fellowship with the Lord Jesus Christ throughout our lives.

Name _____

## Lesson Eighteen          Worksheet

*True or False.*

_____ 1. The first work of the Holy Spirit is to enable Christians to live a Christ-like life.

_____ 2. A Christian is a person who has been set apart for Christ and His service.

_____ 3. Sanctification is the continuous process through which the Holy Spirit makes believers holy in heart and life.

_____ 4. Faith in Christ makes us perfectly holy and sinless.

_____ 5. We are completely justified and forgiven as soon as we believe.

_____ 6. Our sanctification will be complete only when we are transformed and glorified in heaven.

_____ 7. You must first be saved before you can grow as a Christian.

_____ 8. To grow in grace is to love Jesus Christ more and more as you continue to see how much He has done for you in saving you.

_____ 9. Sanctification has nothing to do with our daily living.

_____ 10. It is only possible to grow as you listen to what God has to say to you in His Word.

_____ 11. The best place to start reading the Bible is in the book of Leviticus.

_____ 12. Prayer to the soul is like air to the body, without it you will die spiritually.

_____ 13. In prayer we talk to God only about our needs.

_____ 14. Church attendance is not really very important in spiritual growth.

_____ 15. The Christian will not be affected by the books or magazines he reads.

_____ 16. When we witness to the unsaved we should make sure they know they are wrong.

_____ 17. Growth comes as Christians read the Bible, pray, worship and witness.

_____ 18. The Holy Spirit can sanctify you even if you resist His work in your life.

_____ 19. God does not want your life and actions to be like those of the unsaved.

_____ 20. After you become a Christian, the devil will no longer tempt you to sin.

_____ 21. After you become a Christian, you will not have any desire to sin against God.

_____ 22. We really have no power of our own to fight against the temptations of the devil, but the Holy Spirit will give us power to resist the devil.

_____ 23. The Bible tells us as Christians that we can live pretty much as we please.

_____ 24. Most of the sin in our lives begins with our thoughts.

_____ 25. When you sin as a Christian, you should immediately return to Jesus Christ to confess your sin.

*Completion Questions.*

26. Explain the difference between sanctification in the broad sense and in the narrow sense.

27. Compare physical growth and spiritual growth in a person.

28. Why is it important to read the Bible and pray every day?

29. What should Christians do when they sense the temptations of the devil?

30. Explain the two natures of a Christian.

*Answer the following questions from your study of Acts 19.*

31. What happened when some Jews tried to drive out evil spirits?

32. What was Demetrius' occupation, and why did he oppose Paul's preaching?

33. Who settled the uprising of the Jews, and how did he do it?

---

# The Holy Christian Church

*Assignment*

Read Acts 20. Review the Third Article and its meaning and study questions 237-246 in the *Explanation of Luther's Small Catechism*. Read this lesson, complete the worksheet and be prepared for a quiz.

*Christ loved the church and gave himself up for her to make her holy, cleansing her by the washing with water through the word, and to present her to himself as a radiant church, without stain or wrinkle or any other blemish, but holy and blameless. Ephesians 5:25b-27*

## The Third Article of the Apostles' Creed

"I believe in the Holy Spirit, the holy Christian church, the communion of saints, the forgiveness of sins, the resurrection of the body, and the life everlasting. Amen."

The explanation to the Third Article says, I believe that...the Holy Spirit...calls, gathers, enlightens and sanctifies the whole Christian church on earth, and preserves it in union with Jesus Christ in the one true faith,

163

in which Christian church He daily forgives abundantly all my sins, and the sins of all believers..."

## The Holy Christian Church

The beginning of the church is recorded in Acts 2. Here we read that the church was born on Pentecost, fifty days after Easter Sunday, or just ten days after Jesus ascended into heaven.

The church is found wherever the gospel is rightly taught and where the sacraments are rightly administered. The church is called the *workmanship* (Ephesians 2:10) of the Holy Spirit because He produces the church by bringing people to faith in the Lord Jesus Christ and making them members of His body. It may also be called His *workshop* because it is the body in which He works to produce sanctified Christians.

The church is called *holy* because the Holy Spirit works in and through the church. It is called holy because its head, the Lord Jesus Christ, is holy, and because the means of grace are holy. And finally the church is called holy because its true members lead holy lives, and because they are to be perfected in heaven. It is called Christian because its true membership believes in Christ as Savior.

In the creed we confess that we believe in the *holy Christian church.* It would also be proper to call it *the holy catholic church.* However, the word *catholic* does not refer to the Roman Catholic Church. Here the word *catholic* means *universal* or *general.* The Christian church is catholic in this sense. It is a universal or world-wide church in that it is to be found wherever there are true Christian believers. All believers in the Lord Jesus

Christ belong to the *holy Christian church.* This is the only one and true church to be found upon the face of the earth.

## The Communion of Saints

The communion of saints is another name for the Christian church. Saints is the scriptural name for all believers in Christ. It does not mean that they are perfect and sinless. It means that they trust in Christ alone for salvation, have received His forgiveness, are justified by faith in Him, are filled and guided by the Holy Spirit and dedicated to His service.

*Saints* - What is a saint? As the Bible uses this word, it does not refer just to godly people who have been dead for hundreds of years. Rather, it refers to all who have become Christians, to those who are saved (Romans 1:7 and I Corinthians 1:2). A saint is a person who has been made a Christian by the Spirit of God. If you are saved, then the Bible calls you a saint. The word saint is simply another name for a Christian. Every Christian is a saint.

*Communion* - The word *communion* in the Apostle's Creed does not refer specifically to the Sacrament of the Lord's Supper. This word refers rather to the fellowship or kinship which the members of the church enjoy with one another. The holy Christian church is a communion of saints. It is a fellowship of the saints who are members of the church. Christians are partners in Christian faith and love, in spiritual life, and in the hope of eternal salvation. The communion of saints includes also the members of the victorious church in heaven.

# The Saints Are the Church

When we think of the church, a number of ideas come to the minds of people. The church is often thought of as being a building. Some people think of it as being a denomination. Others think of it as just being a particular congregation. There are those who think of it as being some sort of special club or agency. These are mistaken ideas of what the church really is.

The word *church* is used one hundred and fifteen times in the New Testament. In all of these places it refers to people. The Greek word for church is *ekklesia*, which means *the called out ones*. It never has reference to a building or to a particular form of worship. The church is made up of people. According to Acts 2, we learn that the true church is made up of people in whose lives the Holy Spirit has been able to bring about repentance for sin and a living faith in Christ.

# The State of the Church

The entire church, existing through all time and eternity, is made up of those believers who are still alive on earth and of those who have gone to their eternal reward in heaven.

*Church Militant* - The church on earth is called *militant,* because its members are still fighting the good fight of faith. They are still struggling against the devil, the world and their own flesh.

*Church Triumphant* - The church in heaven is called *triumphant,* because its members have won the victory of faith.

It is essentially the same church on earth and in heaven. It is one body with one head, Christ Jesus. The entrance into the Church Triumphant is through the Church Militant. The congregation of the saints in heaven is made up of those who have been saints or believers on earth. Here on earth the believers are in a state of imperfect sanctification. In heaven they are transformed and glorified into the likeness of Christ their Savior.

## The Visible and Invisible Church

The terms visible and invisible are used to describe the form of the church. However, they are not entirely accurate because there are not two churches. Rather the terms refer to two aspects of the same church. One (invisible) refers to its inner reality and the other (visible) to its outward manifestation upon earth.

*Visible* - The church is often spoken of as being *visible* because people who are Christians can certainly be seen. But whenever Christians come together as a congregation of the church, hypocrites (people who pretend to be Christians) may also join the congregation. However, these people are not members of the true Christian Church. Only God finally knows who are the true members of His church. The visible church is the organized church upon earth. An example of the visible church is your own local congregation.

*Invisible* - The church is often spoken of as being *invisible* because we cannot look into the lives of other people and judge whether they are true believers in Christ or not. The invisible church consists of all true believers and saints on earth and in heaven. It is the organism and living body of which Christ is the head. Therefore, the invisible church is made up only of those, living or dead, who truly know Christ as Savior.

## Are You a Member of the Church?

This is an important question for you to answer. You are a member of the true church of Christ if you have allowed the Holy Spirit to work true repentance and faith in your soul. The great tragedy is that people can belong to the outward or visible church organization without being members of the true church of Christ. Today the Holy Spirit calls you to examine yourself to see if you are really a member of the true church of Jesus Christ.

Name _____

## Lesson Nineteen      **Worksheet**

*True or False.*

_____ 1. The beginning of the church is recorded in the book of Genesis.

_____ 2. In Genesis we read that the church was born on the first day of creation.

_____ 3. The true church is found only where the gospel is rightly taught and where the sacraments are rightly administered.

_____ 4. The Holy Spirit is not really needed in the work of the church.

_____ 5. The church is called holy because its head, Jesus Christ, is holy.

_____ 6. The church is called holy because its members lead holy lives.

_____ 7. The word *catholic* refers to the church we call the Roman Catholic Church.

_____ 8. The church is called *universal* or *world-wide* in that it is found wherever there are true Christian believers.

_____ 9. All believers in Christ belong to the *holy Christian church.*

_____ 10. The church is called Christian because its true membership believes in Christ as Savior.

_____ 11. *Saints* is a scriptural term used only for certain great Christians.

_____ 12. Only if you live a real godly life will you be called a saint.

_____ 13. Every Christian is a saint.

_____ 14. The word *communion* in the Apostles' Creed refers to the Lord's Supper.

_____ 15. The communion of saints also includes the members of the church in heaven.

_____ 16. The true church is the building in which we gather to worship the Lord.

_____ 17. Some think of the church as being some sort of a special club or agency.

_____ 18. The word *church* is not found often in the New Testament.

_____ 19. Hypocrites may be members of the true Christian church.

169

_____ 20. The true church consists of only true believers who are living on earth.

_____ 21. The church on earth is called *Triumphant* because its members have won the victory of faith.

_____ 22. The entrance into the Church Triumphant is through the Church Militant.

_____ 23. The visible church consists only of Christians who are true believers.

_____ 24. The invisible church includes all true believers on earth and in heaven.

_____ 25. You are a member of the true church of Jesus Christ only if you have allowed the Holy Spirit to work true repentance and faith in your soul.

*Completion Questions.*

26. The church was born on _____ , which was _____ days after _____.

27. Why is the church called the workmanship of the Holy Spirit?

28. According to the Bible, what is a saint?

29. What is the church according to Acts 2?

30. What is meant by the term *Church Militant*?

*Answer the following questions from your study of Acts 20.*

31. What happened one night while Paul was speaking, and what did he do about it?

32. How did Paul respond to the hardships which the Holy Spirit warned him about?

33. Why did Paul tell the Ephesian overseers to be shepherds of the church of God?

# The Work of the Church

## Assignment

Read Acts 21. Review the Third Article and its meaning and study questions 247-255 in the *Explanation of Luther's Small Catechism*. Read this lesson, complete the worksheet and be prepared for a quiz.

*Therefore go and make disciples of all nations, baptizing them in the name of the Father and of the Son and of the Holy Spirit, and teaching them to obey everything I have commanded you. And surely I will be with you always, to the very end of the age. Matthew 28:19-20*

### The Third Article of the Apostles' Creed

"I believe in the Holy Spirit, the holy Christian church, the communion of saints, the forgiveness of sins, the resurrection of the body, and the life everlasting. Amen."

In the Apostles' Creed we confess that we believe in the Holy Spirit who has brought into being the Holy Christian church. This Christian church is also called the communion of saints (believers). He provides them moment by moment with the forgiveness of sins, and will

171

some day raise them from the dead to life everlasting. This work of the Holy Spirit is called *sanctification*, using the word in the broad sense.

## The Holy Christian Church

We confess that we believe in the holy Christian church when we recite the words of the Apostles' Creed. As we stated in our last lesson, there is only one true church on earth, the holy Christian church. This church consists of all who know Jesus Christ as Savior. We become saints as we hear the Word of God and the Holy Spirit through that Word brings us to repentance and faith. Remember, the moment the Holy Spirit works repentance and faith in us, we are immediately regenerated, justified, converted and saved. This is all the work of the Holy Spirit in us.

The instant the Holy Spirit has worked repentance and faith in us, we find ourselves *in Christ*. We are then members of "... the church, which is his body" (Ephesians 1:22,23). The church is a body of people who have been saved from sin. It is a body of people who have become children of God through the work of the Holy Spirit.

## The Church Begins

As we stated in our last lesson, the church came into being on the Jewish festival called the *Pentecost*. It was fifty days after the resurrection of Jesus Christ from the dead and ten days after Jesus ascended into heaven. On this day, the Holy Spirit came to earth to dwell within those who believed in the Lord Jesus Christ. We speak of the day of Pentecost as the day the church was born. This day is the birthday of the Christian church.

The church began with about one hundred and twenty members who had something in common. They had all been filled with the same Holy Spirit on the day of Pentecost. They were all saved and empowered now to be witnesses for Jesus Christ. They were all born of the Spirit of God. The Spirit of Jesus had come to live in them. On that same day, about three thousand more people became members of the holy Christian church. All this took place in the city of Jerusalem. This became the first Christian congregation of the church.

## The Growth of the Church

During the first couple of centuries after the founding of the church in Jerusalem, Christians brought the good news of Jesus Christ to many countries. As this good news spread, people were brought to faith in Jesus Christ. These same people banded together into congregations or churches. There really were no denominational names to these churches. They were simply known as the church in such and such a particular city or country. They were bodies or groups of believers who had experienced the work of the Holy Spirit in their lives, the work of repentance and faith. As more and more believers came together, the church grew. This took place as "the Lord added to their number daily those who were being saved (Acts 2:47).

As time went on, the organized church began to accept more government for itself. At first each congregation ruled itself through its spiritual leaders. Later some of these spiritual leaders (pastors and bishops) began to exercise authority and guidance over more than one congregation.

*Years 30-100 A.D.* - During this time most congregations were self ruling by their own congregational leadership. Guidance was given by the apostles who were still living. The Apostle John was probably the last apostle to die (approximately 100 A.D.). He wrote the Gospel of John, the three Epistles of John, and the book of Revelation.

*Years 100-590 A.D.* - During this time there was a growing tendency for some pastors or bishops to exercise power or guidance over a number of congregations. The bishops in the following cities became prominent in their power: Rome, Constantinople, Alexandria, Antioch and Jerusalem. Toward the end of this period, the two most powerful bishops were the ones at Rome and Constantinople.

By the year 590, the organized church in the city of Rome had a good deal of influence and power over all the other churches in the world. About this time, we begin to speak of the organized church as being the Roman Church with the pope as its head.

*Years 590-1054 A.D.* - Outwardly, the church remained somewhat unified, but the popes of Rome and the patriarchs of Constantinople were trying to rule each other. Finally in the year 1054, the first major break took place in the organized church as the two powers split. The pope in Rome excommunicated the patriarch of the church in Constantinople. Immediately this patriarch sent back a letter of excommunication to the pope in Rome excommunicating him and the churches under him. Since that time, the church at Rome ruled by the pope has been known as the Latin or Roman Catholic Church, while the church at Constantinople, ruled by the patriarch, has been known as the Greek Orthodox Church. This split remains today.

*Years 1054-1517 A.D.* - The second major break took place within the Roman Catholic Church on October 31, 1517, when Martin Luther nailed his theses to the door of the Castle Church in Wittenberg, Germany. This was the beginning of what is called *The Protestant Reformation.* Luther's theses were ninety-five statements, nearly all objecting to the sale of *indulgences.* These statements struck at the authority of the pope and the priesthood of the Roman Church.

Within a few years, the followers of Martin Luther were condemned by the Roman Church. From that time on these followers were called *Protestants,* and their doctrines became known as those representing the Protestant faith. The Protestant Reformation was a back-to-the-Bible movement.

This Protestant Reformation and break with the Roman Church quickly spread to other European countries such as Switzerland, Denmark, Sweden, Norway, France and England. As the Protestant faith spread in these various countries, people became followers of such men as Martin Luther, John Calvin, Ulric Zwingli and John Knox.

As time went on, these followers formed into various church organizations or denominations, most of them being known as Protestants. The denominations which were formed in the early years of the Reformation were the Lutherans, the Presbyterians, the Reformed churches of Germany and Holland, the Anglican Church in

England and the various Baptist churches. At a still later time, the Methodist churches came into being as a result of another reformation movement within the Anglican Church in England. John Wesley and his brother, Charles, were instrumental in this movement.

*Years 1517 to the present time* - The Greek Church and the Roman Church continue to live and grow. The Reformation produced many Protestant churches—one of which is the Lutheran Church.

*The Lutheran Church* - Many true believers began to gather under the leadership of Martin Luther in the year 1517. Later, these believers began to call themselves *Lutherans*. Martin Luther strongly opposed the use of this name, but he was unable to prevent it from happening. Today Lutheran congregations are found in many places of the world. The task set before the Lutheran Church is still the same, "make disciples of all nations, baptizing them...and teaching them..." (Matthew 28:19).

Historically, the Lutheran Church has believed in the entire Scripture as the only rule and standard of faith and practice. To this the Roman Church added tradition. The Lutheran Church teaches that people are saved by faith alone without works. The Roman Church teaches that people are saved by faith and works. The Lutheran Church abides by the Word of God even when she cannot understand it. She does not reject or explain away the teachings of Scripture because they seem unreasonable.

## The Work of the Church

The work of the church is briefly described by Jesus in His last message as recorded in Matthew 28:19-20, "Therefore go and make disciples of all nations, baptizing them in the name of the Father and of the Son and of the Holy Spirit, and teaching them to obey everything I have commanded you..." The church is the instrument which the Holy Spirit uses for the evangelization of the world, for "making disciples of all nations." This is to be accomplished by baptizing and teaching. This is no small task. The Holy Spirit gives gifts and spiritual power to the Christians that He might speak through them and offer salvation to all. Often the organized church has failed greatly in this task. At other times the church has gone forward to the glory of God.

## Congregations Banded Together

Why have congregations banded together in synods? They have usually done so to more effectively carry out the work which Christ has given to the church. For example, leadership in the form of pastors is needed. It would be impossible for one congregation to set up its own seminary for the training of its pastors. However, when a number of congregations do this together, then it becomes possible to have colleges, seminaries and other schools.

The same is true in the task of world mission and home mission work. When many congregations band together they are able to train and send out missionaries to many parts of the world.

## The Church Is One

While the church is one, the outward congregational organization of the church has become divided into many different groups and denominations. Today, some of the main branches of the organized church are: The Roman Church; The Orthodox Church; The Lutheran Church; The Reformed Churches. The last two churches are called Protestant because they *protested* against the false teachings and practices which had crept into the church.

In spite of these many and various divisions within the organized church, there is still only one holy Christian church upon earth. This church is made up of members who truly belong to Jesus Christ. These people may be found in many areas or organizations of the organized church which is to be looked upon as the body of Christ.

People who belong to Jesus Christ will most often join in the fellowship of a congregation, which is immediately an outward organization of the church. The organized church must always remember that it exists to edify and strengthen the believers, to help the sick and the needy, and to pray. However, the main purpose of the church, according to Matthew 28:18-20, is to make disciples of all nations.

Are you a member of the one true Christian church? Are you actively involved in this great work? Remember, you are either a missionary or a mission field.

# Lesson Twenty          Worksheet

*True or False.*

_____ 1. In the Apostles' Creed, we confess that we believe the Holy Spirit has brought the Christian church into being.

_____ 2. The holy Christian church is also called the communion of saints.

_____ 3. The holy Christian church is made up of all true believers.

_____ 4. Only those who know Jesus Christ as Savior are members of the holy Christian church.

_____ 5. We become saints if we live a good life and do great works.

_____ 6. We will never be sure we are saved until we die.

_____ 7. The Bible calls the church a body.

_____ 8. The church came into being on Easter Sunday at Christ's resurrection.

_____ 9. The church began with twelve charter members, the twelve apostles.

_____ 10. The first Christian congregation of the church was in Rome.

_____ 11. The first congregations were ruled by district leaders or bishops.

_____ 12. The Apostle Paul was probably the last apostle to die, around 100 A. D.

_____ 13. By the year 590 A. D. the church in Jerusalem had a good deal of influence and power over all the other churches in the world.

_____ 14. The church at Constantinople is known as the Greek Orthodox Church.

_____ 15. The second major break took place in the church on October 31, 1751.

_____ 16. Luther's ninety-five theses objected to the sale of indulgences.

_____ 17. The followers of Martin Luther were welcomed by the Roman Catholic Church.

_____ 18. The Protestant Reformation was really a back-to-the-Bible movement.

179

_____ 19. The Lutheran Church came into being in the early years of the Reformation.

_____ 20. Luther encouraged his followers to call themselves Lutherans.

_____ 21. There is really not much difference between the teachings of the Lutheran Church and the Roman Catholic Church.

_____ 22. The Lutheran Church believes in the entire Scripture as the only rule and standard of faith and practice.

_____ 23. The work of the church is briefly described by Jesus in Matthew 28:18-20.

_____ 24. The Holy Spirit empowers the Christian to be a witness for Christ.

_____ 25. While the organized church has become divided, the true church is *one*.

*Completion Questions.*

26. When was the first major break in the organized church, and what happened??

27. How did the Protestant Reformation begin?

28. Who are the Protestants and how did they get this name?

29. Give two reasons why congregations are more effective in banding together.

   a.

   b.

30. What is the main purpose of the church?

*Answer the following questions from your study of Acts 21.*

31. What did Paul say when the disciples pleaded with him not to go up to Jerusalem?

32. What report did Paul give to the brethren at Jerusalem?

33. How was Paul rescued from the people who dragged him from the temple and who were trying to kill him?

# The Forgiveness Of Sins

*Assignment*

Read Acts 22. Review the Third Article and its meaning and study questions 256-264 in the *Explanation of Luther's Small Catechism*. Read this lesson, complete the worksheet and be prepared for a quiz.

*If you, O Lord, kept a record of sins, O Lord, who could stand? But with you there is forgiveness; therefore you are feared. Psalm 130:3-4*

## The Third Article of the Apostles' Creed

"I believe in the Holy Spirit, the holy Christian church, the communion of saints, the forgiveness of sins, the resurrection of the body, and the life everlasting. Amen."

The explanation to the Third Article says, "I believe that I cannot by my own reason or strength believe in Jesus Christ, my Lord, or come to Him, but the Holy Spirit has called me through the Gospel....in which Christian church He daily forgives abundantly all my sins, and the sins of all believers..."

We confess that we believe in "the forgiveness of sins." However, it is possible to confess these words and yet not be sure that we have been forgiven all of our sins. This may be because we have not claimed God's forgiveness. We may have honestly confessed our sins to God and still we do not have the assurance that God has forgiven us. In this case we need to take God at His word, which is to believe that He will do what He has promised (Ephesians 1:7: I John 1:9). This is to act upon the promises of God.

## The Holy Spirit Calls

The Holy Spirit calls us through the Means of Grace: the Word and the Sacraments. Through the Law He shows us our sin and what will happen if we do not repent and turn in faith to Jesus Christ, the One who has purchased pardon and forgiveness for all our sins. Through the Gospel in the Word and the Sacraments He calls us to faith in Christ. We are not able to believe in Jesus Christ or come to Him by our own understanding or effort. However, the Holy Spirit calls us to believe in Jesus and come to Him. When He brings us to faith in Jesus, then we immediately receive, as a free gift from God, the forgiveness of sins.

Martin Luther, after he was saved, wrote a personal testimony of his faith in Christ and how he came to this faith. This testimony is found in his explanations of the Three Articles of the Apostles' Creed. In his testimony of faith as expressed in his explanation of the Third Article, he states, "I believe that I cannot by my own reason or strength believe in Jesus Christ my Lord, or come to Him, but the Holy Spirit has called me through the Gospel..."

# Divine Forgiveness

The grace of God's forgiveness is offered us in Jesus Christ. He alone has acquired it for us by His sinless obedience and atoning death. Through Him, grace is given to every believer. The Holy Spirit makes it ours through faith which He creates and preserves in our hearts.

Christ became our sin-bearer. He took upon Himself our sin and our guilt, so that when we come before God, clothed in the righteousness of Christ, our sin is not counted against us. We are acquitted, that is, declared free. Not guilty is the verdict. We are justified and forgiven through faith in Christ.

It was customary in ancient times to throw a debtor into prison. If another paid the bill, the debtor would be released. The merit of another was counted as though it were the debtor's. A lamb was most frequently used as the sacrifice. The priest laid his hand upon the lamb offered for sin, and while the sinner confessed sin over the head of the sacrifice, the sin was typically transferred to the victim, which was therefore called sin or guilt. Thus God laid upon His Son the iniquities of us all. As St. Paul said, "God made him who had no sin to be sin for us, so that in him we might become the righteousness of God" (II Corinthians 5:21).

In Lesson Sixteen, justification was defined as an act of God by which, for the sake of the obedience of Christ in our place, He graciously and freely forgives the sinner who believes in Christ as Savior, and regards that one as righteous. When God looks upon us in Christ, He no longer sees our own guilt and unrighteousness but the righteousness of Christ which we put on by faith.

## Daily Forgiveness

The forgiveness of sin is received daily and abundantly through the means of grace. Although we are completely forgiven, forgiveness is not received once and for all. It is like the light of the sun coming to us every day. It is like the air we breathe continually. As we need this light and air all along to maintain our physical life and health, so we need God's forgiving grace for the preservation of our spiritual life and health.

We are sinful and we sin every day. We often fail to do what we ought to do and we often do what we ought not do. Unconsciously and unintentionally, or surprised by the tempter in a moment of weakness or unwatchfulness, we commit many sins. We therefore need daily forgiveness. Forgiveness is what the Holy Spirit brings to every repentant person who confesses sin and in faith believes the promises in God's Word.

Sorrow will not restore or bring back what has been lost. Tears will not wash away the consequences of foolishness. Regret will not bring back the lost opportunity. God must remove sin if it is to be removed, and this act of His wondrous mercy He does at the throne of grace. There is no need to despair. God has made provision, Christ has made atonement, and the Holy Spirit brings this forgiveness to us through His means of grace.

## Complete Forgiveness

God never forgives people for a part of their sins. He either forgives them all or He forgives none of them. Forgiveness is a personal matter. God forgives the sinner. Strictly speaking He does not forgive the sins, but He forgives sinners of their sins. God can never look with favor upon sin but He does look with favor upon the repentant and believing sinner. Therefore, either the sinner is forgiven and reconciled with God, or else the sinner is unforgiven and unreconciled. Either a person has been received as a child of God, or has not been so received. There is no such thing as a partial forgiveness, a partial reconciliation, or a partial sonship.

The believer cannot be regarded with favor and counted righteous if even a single sin remained unforgiven. But God forgives all who believe. He casts all sin behind His back and He no longer sees them (Isaiah 38:17). When people think that God has forgiven them all their sins, but not this one or that one, they are either under a delusion which robs them of the inward peace they might otherwise have, or the sin which they fear is not forgiven, is one which they have not sincerely repented of, and are still shielding and cherishing. Genuine contrition and faith are followed by free and complete forgiveness.

When we receive Jesus Christ as Savior, all our sins are forgiven. The prodigal son apparently went to the extreme limit of sin, yet when he repented and came back, he was received and forgiven. Peter committed a most grievous sin against his Lord when he denied Him, but when he sought forgiveness, he found it. God has promised, "If we confess our sins, he is faithful and just and will forgive us our sins and purify us from all unrighteousness" (I John 1:9).

## Personal Forgiveness

The central teaching of the Bible is that all who believe, receive the forgiveness of their sins and are justified before God; not by works, but by grace, for

Christ's sake, through faith. After all, there are only two religions in the world, God's and man's. Man's religion is always based on self-righteousness. God's religion is based on Jesus' blood and righteousness. Man's religion says, first you must do, then you shall live. God's religion says, first you must live by grace through faith in Christ, then you shall do. Man's religion says you are saved by character. God's religion says you are saved by grace in Christ alone.

We can fall from grace and be lost. But if we abide in Christ, are faithful to His Word, trust in His grace, desire to do His will, accept daily forgiveness, and have a forgiving spirit, we may rest assured in the promise that, ". . . neither height nor depth, nor anything else in all creation, will be able to separate us from the love of God that is in Christ Jesus our Lord" (Romans 8:39).

Are you abiding in Christ and in His forgiveness?

# Lesson Twenty-One     Worksheet

*True or False.*

_____ 1. In the Third Article we confess that we believe in the forgiveness of sin.

_____ 2. Some people are not sure that God has forgiven all of their sins.

_____ 3. Everyone who confesses sin to God is sure of being forgiven.

_____ 4. We need to believe the promise of God to have the assurance of forgiveness.

_____ 5. The Holy Spirit shows us our sin and what will happen if we do not repent and turn in faith to Jesus Christ.

_____ 6. We are able to believe in Jesus Christ by our own understanding.

_____ 7. The Holy Spirit calls us to believe in Jesus and to come to Him.

_____ 8. When we come to Jesus, we sometimes have to wait to be forgiven of our sin.

_____ 9. Martin Luther's testimony of his faith in Christ is found in his explanation of the Ten Commandments.

_____ 10. Martin Luther believed he was able to come to Christ in his own strength.

_____ 11. We can be forgiven only because of Jesus' sinless obedience and atoning death.

_____ 12. All are forgiven by Christ whether they believe or not.

_____ 13. Even though we are forgiven by Christ, we must bear the guilt of our sin.

_____ 14. Jesus became sin for us, that we might be made the righteousness of God.

_____ 15. When God looks upon us in Christ, He no longer sees our sin.

_____ 16. We receive the forgiveness of God once and for all when we are saved.

_____ 17. We are dependent upon God's forgiving grace for the preservation of our spiritual life.

_____ 18. Because we are sinful and we sin every day, we need daily forgiveness.

_____ 19. If we are sorry enough for our sin, our sin will be removed from us.

_____ 20. Our tears will wash away the consequences of our sinfulness.

_____ 21. At times, God forgives us for only some of our sins.

_____ 22. God will not look with favor upon us if a single sin is unforgiven.

_____ 23. If we confess our sins, Jesus is faithful and just to forgive us our sins.

_____ 24. The religion of the Bible is based on Jesus' blood and righteousness.

_____ 25. It is impossible for us to fall from grace and be lost.

*Completion Questions.*

26. Why are some people not sure that God has forgiven them?

27. What does the Holy Spirit show us through the Law, and in the Gospel?

28. How is forgiveness a personal matter?

29. What promise is given in I John 1:9?

30. How is God's religion different from man's religion?

*Answer the following questions from your study of Acts 22.*

31. Briefly tell the story of Paul's conversion.

32. According to Ananias, what had God chosen Paul to be?

33. Why was the centurion afraid to beat Paul?

# The Resurrection of the Body

*Assignment*

Read Acts 23. Review the Third Article and its meaning and study questions 265-272 in the *Explanation of Luther's Small Catechism*. Read this lesson, complete the worksheet and be prepared for a quiz.

*Jesus said to her, "I am the resurrection and the life. He who believes in me will live, even though he dies; and whoever lives and believes in me will never die. Do you believe this?" John 11:25-26*

## The Third Article of the Apostles' Creed

"I believe in the Holy Spirit, the holy Christian church, the communion of saints, the forgiveness of sins, the resurrection of the body, and the life everlasting. Amen."

The explanation to the Third Article says, "I believe that I cannot by my own reason or strength believe in Jesus Christ, my Lord, or come to Him but the Holy Spirit has called me through the Gospel...and at the last day will raise up me and all the dead, and will grant everlasting life to me and to all who believe in Christ. This is most certainly true."

When we believe and confess that the Holy Spirit will raise the dead, we realize that in a unique way He is the Spirit of God and of Christ. For in the Bible the resurrection of the dead is attributed to God and Christ.

## The Resurrection and Eternal Life

The separation which takes place at death between the soul and the body is not permanent. There will be a resurrection of the dead when the soul and the body will be reunited.

Eternal life begins here on earth, in time, and not at death. But at death the soul of the Christian will enter into the full and perfect joy of heaven. Only through the saving grace of God will we experience the blessedness of being like Christ. Our peace will then pass all understanding. We will be forever satisfied because we will be free from sin and all evil. As we read in the Psalms, "And I—in righteousness I will see your face; when I awake, I will be satisfied with seeing your likeness" (Psalm 17:15).

The unbelieving and impenitent, the unsaved, will be cast away from the presence of the Lord to live in the torments of hell. This end is the eternal consequence of rejecting Christ. The deeper their sin, the deeper their anguish and regret. Unfit for heaven, they will be cast into the realm of Satan with those who have served him and become like him. But no one who has received God's gift of salvation will be lost.

# The Teaching of Scripture

The doctrine of the resurrection of the body is a scriptural one. Even though it was denied by many in the days of the apostles and is denied by many today, it is a doctrine that is clearly and definitely taught in the Bible.

Isaiah said that the dead shall live (Isaiah 26:19). Daniel declared that those who "sleep in the dust of the earth will awake: some to everlasting life, some to shame and everlasting contempt" (Daniel 12:2). The belief in the resurrection was common among the Jews even though the Sadducees denied it.

In the New Testament Jesus said, "Do not be amazed at this, for a time is coming when all who are in their graves will hear his voice and come out—those who have done good will rise to live, and those who have done evil will rise to be condemned (John 5:28-29). Those who are raised from the dead shall neither marry nor die any more and shall be equal unto the angels (Luke 20:35-36).

## The Nature of the Resurrection

The resurrection of the dead will be a real resurrection of all the bodies of the dead, both of the just and the unjust. Such a bodily resurrection is necessary in order that believers and unbelievers may, as complete human beings with body and soul, receive the award of eternal life or eternal death.

## The Nature of the Body

What the resurrection body will be like is learned from the example of the risen body of Christ in whose likeness

191

our bodies will be made, and also from the description of the resurrection body given by the apostle Paul. It will be our own body so that we and others will recognize it as our own, but it will have new properties and powers. This does not necessarily mean that every particle of matter that made up the body at death will be present in it at the resurrection. In this life we recognize our body as our own, although we know that it is constantly changing, and that at the end of every seven years, it is made up of new particles of matter. In the same way it is possible for the resurrection body to be the same body as we had on earth, even though it should be made up of entirely different particles.

The body of Christ, after His resurrection, was His own body and was recognized by His disciples. However, it possessed new attributes and powers. It was freed from the limitations of space in that it could go through closed doors and appear and disappear as He willed. Being a spiritual body, it was not limited as our physical bodies are. It was freed from the weaknesses and limitations of the natural body. This new spiritual body will thus be given new and wonderful powers.

Our present body is of the earth, but the resurrection body will be heavenly (I Corinthians 15:47-49). Such a change is necessary because flesh and blood cannot inherit the kingdom of God. For this reason the believer, though forgiven, dies, that through death and the resurrection a new body may be brought from the grave. The bodies of those who are alive at Christ's second coming will be changed in a moment, in the twinkling of an eye (I Corinthians 15:51-53). The bodies of all the believers will be made fit tabernacles for their redeemed and glorified souls.

The resurrection bodies will have the following attributes: they will be immortal, will not die; and be incorruptible, cannot sin. They will be glorious, perfect and powerful, free from all diseases, sufferings and defects of the earthly body. The bodies of the unbelievers will also be changed, but doomed to eternal destruction.

## The Blessedness of Heaven

The blessedness of heaven consists in this:

1. *We shall see God "face to face."* The Apostle John said, "But we know that when he appears, we shall be like him, for we shall see him as he is" (I John 3:2b). We shall eternally enjoy the beautiful vision of looking at the face of Jesus.

2. *We shall know the angels.* We shall know all the saints of the past. We will meet the patriarchs, Abraham, Isaac, Jacob, etc.; the prophets, Isaiah, Daniel, Jonah, etc.; the apostles including Peter, James, John; and all our Christian friends.

3. *We shall be clothed with the divine image.* Our intellect will be enlightened. Our will will be obedient to God's will. Our heart will be in love with all that is good. As we read in scripture, "We shall be like him" (I John 3:2).

4. *We shall be free from all ills.* There will be no sin, no sorrow, and no death. There will be no unfulfilled wants and desires. There will be no troubles.

5. *We shall receive degrees of glory.* Greater glory is given as a reward, not of merit, but of grace to those who on earth showed their faith in consecrated service to the Lord and in many good works done to their neighbors.

In heaven there will be no earthly conditions and customs, no division into families, no civil governments, no earthly vocations, no church divisions and no mission work (Mark 12:25).

Because Jesus rose from the dead, He gives His resurrection power and promise of heaven to all who know Him as Savior. Do you know Him? Your eternal destiny will be either heaven or hell, and it will be determined by what you have done with Jesus. As he said, "Whoever believes in the Son has eternal life, but whoever rejects the Son will not see life, for God's wrath remains on him" (John 3:36).

# Lesson Twenty-Two    Worksheet

*True or False.*

_____ 1. In the Third Article, we confess that we are spiritually help-less.

_____ 2. In the Third Article, we confess that the Holy Spirit will raise the dead.

_____ 3. The separation at death between the soul and the body is permanent.

_____ 4. The soul and the body will be reunited at the resurrection.

_____ 5. Eternal life begins only when we get to heaven.

_____ 6. The Christian will enter into the full and perfect joy of heaven at the moment of death.

_____ 7. If we try hard enough, we can attain to the likeness of Christ.

_____ 8. In heaven, every prayer will be finally and fully answered.

_____ 9. The unbelievers will be unafraid to stand in the presence of the Lord.

_____ 10. Hell will be the eternal consequence of rejecting Christ.

_____ 11. The resurrection of the body was accepted by everyone in the days of the apostles and is accepted by everyone today.

_____ 12. The scriptural teaching of the resurrection is found only in the New Testament.

_____ 13. The Bible tells us that in heaven people will marry and have families.

_____ 14. A bodily resurrection is necessary for complete human beings with body and soul to receive the award of eternal life or eternal death.

_____ 15. The cause of the resurrection will be the natural human power to survive.

_____ 16. Our resurrected bodies will be like the body of the risen Christ.

_____ 17. We will recognize others and ourselves in our resurrected bodies.

_____ 18. The body of Christ, after His resurrection, was His own body.

195

_____ 19. The resurrected body of Christ could go through closed doors and appear and disappear as He willed.

_____ 20. The resurrection bodies will be perfect, immortal and incorruptible.

_____ 21. The resurrected bodies of the unbelievers will have all the same properties which belong to those of the believers.

_____ 22. We will know in heaven only those we knew here on earth.

_____ 23. In heaven there will be no sickness, no sorrow, no sin, no troubles.

_____ 24. Rewards will be given in heaven to those who faithfully served the Lord.

_____ 25. Only because Jesus rose from the dead will we one day rise from the dead.

*Completion Questions.*

26. How can we know that there will be a resurrection from the dead?

27. How can we know what our resurrected bodies will be like?

28. Why is a resurrected body necessary to enter heaven?

29. What will the resurrected body be like?

a.

b.

c.

d.

e.

f.

30. Why is heaven a blessed place?

a.

b.

c.

*Answer the following questions from your study of Acts 23.*

31. What was the reason for the dispute between the Pharisees and the Sadducees?

32. How did Paul find out about the plot to kill him?

33. Why did the commander rescue Paul and send him to Felix?

# Unit II Test

## The Third Article

*Assignment*

Review the text and the worksheets for lessons 14-22 in this book. Review all the memory assignments in the *Explanation of Luther's Small Catechism,* questions 206-272. Know the Third Article, its meaning, and the following questions well: 209, 212, 214, 218, 222, 228, 230, 232, 233, 234, 238, 256, 261, 262 and 268. Review Acts 15-23.

*And this is the testimony: God has given us eternal life, and this life is in his Son. He who has the Son has life; He who does not have the Son of God does not have life. I write these things to you who believe in the name of the Son of God so that you may know that you have eternal life. I John 5:11-13*

# Some Facts to Remember

## *Lesson 14*

- The Holy Spirit is not an *it,* but a person, the third person of the Trinity.
- The Holy Spirit came to live within the disciples on the day of Pentecost.
- Since then all believers receive the gift of the Holy Spirit when they are saved.

## *Lesson 15*

- By nature we are dead in sin with neither desire nor ability to believe in Christ.
- The Holy Spirit calls and awakens us to see our sin through the law.
- Repentance includes a willingness to admit and confess sin, to be sorry about sin, to hate and forsake all sin and a desire to be forgiven.
- Faith is the empty hand which receives the gift of salvation God offers us in Christ through the means of grace. It, too, is a gift from God.

## *Lesson 16*

- Saving faith may be described from these three viewpoints: knowledge, assent, confidence or trust.
- The saving power of faith lies not in the faith itself but in that which faith holds fast, namely, Christ and His merits.

- Justification means that we are forgiven and declared righteous in Christ.

## Lesson 17

- Regeneration is the act of God by which He gives to the repentant sinner new spiritual life. It means "to cause to be reborn, to be born again, spiritually."
- Salvation is the free gift of God given to those in whom the Holy Spirit works true repentance and faith.

## Lesson 18

- To sanctify means *to set apart* or *to hallow*. Sanctification is the continuous process by which the Holy Spirit makes believers holy in heart and life.
- Spiritual growth comes as you read God's Word, partake of the Lord's Supper, remember God's promise given to you in baptism, spend time in prayer, attend worship services and tell others about Jesus.
- The Christian has two natures: the old evil nature and the new spiritual nature.

## Lesson 19

- The church was born on the day of Pentecost, ten days after the ascension.
- The New Testament word for *church* does not mean the building, but the people, those who are believers in Christ.

- The church on earth is *militant,* while the church in heaven is *triumphant.*

## Lesson 20

- The Protestant Reformation began in Germany on October 31, 1517, by Martin Luther.
- The work of the church is to go into all nations and make disciples of all people.
- Churches band together to train workers and to carry out mission work.

## Lesson 21

- Forgiveness is offered us only by Christ's sinless obedience and atoning death.
- Because we are sinful and we sin every day we need forgiveness daily.
- When you receive Christ as your Savior all your sins are forgiven.

## Lesson 22

- There will be a resurrection of the dead when the soul and the body are reunited.
- The resurrection bodies will be immortal, perfect, free from disease and sorrow.
- The blessedness of heaven is in being like Jesus, for then we shall see Him as He is.

# The Sacrament of Baptism

*Assignment*

Read Acts 24. Study questions 330-339 in the *Explanation to Luther's Small Catechism*. Read this lesson, complete the worksheet and be prepared for a quiz.

*He said to them, "Go into all the world and preach the good news to all creation. Whoever believes and is baptized will be saved, but whoever does not believe will be condemned." Mark 16:15-16*

## Our Need of God's Grace

The Bible clearly states that from the moment of conception and birth into this world we are sinners. In Psalm 51:5 we read, "Surely I have been a sinner from birth, sinful from the time my mother conceived me." When Adam and Eve sinned against God, they brought the guilt and judgment of sin upon all future generations of people. Ever since that time, every person who has been born into this world has been born with the natural desire to run away from God. This may be expressed to a greater or lesser degree in different people. Nevertheless, by nature we all find it easer to run away from God than to flee to Him in faith and obedience. We call this nature *original sin.*

We do not have to be very old before we begin to express in outward actions the *original sin* in our souls. Just as soon as we are old enough to have strength to express our own desires we begin to commit acts of sin. The Bible says in Romans 3:23, "For all have sinned and fall short of the glory of God." The prophet expressed it this way, "We all, like sheep, have gone astray, each of us has turned to his own way..." (Isaiah 53:6). Because of this, we need God's grace.

## What Is Grace?

Grace is God's undeserved love, His unmerited favor toward us through Jesus Christ.

Grace has also been defined in the following acrostic:

**G** = God's
**R** = Riches (or redemption)
**A** = At
**C** = Christ's
**E** = Expense

We were born lost and by nature we keep on running away from God. We did not deserve God's love. The Bible tells us that God still loves us. "But God demonstrates his own love for us in this: while we are still sinners, Christ died for us" (Romans 5:8). This is what we mean by the word *grace.* We have not deserved God's love but He still loves us and wants to save us. We have not deserved God's favor, and we never will; yet God still favors us and wants to have a relationship with us.

We must remember that although God loves us, and His grace is freely shared with us, it cost Him much. We have learned that God is a just and a righteous and a holy God. Therefore, He must demand the full punishment for sin. He cannot lightly overlook sin. It must be paid for. Instead of expecting people to pay for their own sins, God has made full payment for all the sins of all people for all time through the death of Jesus Christ upon the cross.

## God's Free Gift

God is in the giving business. We are all born with the natural desire to sin and to commit acts of sin daily but God still wants to give us a free gift. We may think of this gift as being threefold, including: forgiveness of sins; eternal life here and now; and salvation. God wants to forgive our sins, give us eternal life right here and now, and give us salvation from the power of sin now and from the presence of sin in the hereafter. He offers this gift to us free and without cost.

## The Means of Grace

God brings His gift to us through the Means of Grace which are the Word of God and the Sacraments of Baptism and the Lord's Supper. These are the channels or the means which God uses.

*The Bible* - The Word of God is a means through which God brings us the offer of His free gift of forgiveness, eternal life and salvation. The Spirit of God is in the Word. This is what gives it saving power. For this reason the Gospel is, as the apostle Paul says, "the power of God for the salvation of everyone who believes" (Romans 1:16).

*Baptism and The Lord's Supper* - From the Bible we learn of two other means which God uses to bring the offer of His free gift to us. These are Baptism and the Lord's Supper. We call these sacraments. There are only two sacraments. Even in the sacraments the central thing is the Word. It is this which makes them sacraments and means of grace.

## What Is a Sacrament?

A sacrament is a sacred and holy act of God, instituted or commanded by Christ Himself, in which visible elements are used, and through which God offers His free gift to us. The three requirements for a sacred act to be called a sacrament are as follows:

*Instituted by Jesus Christ* - There are many sacred acts which we use in the church but which have not been specifically given by Jesus Christ; for example, the service of confirmation. This has never been given by Christ, but is nevertheless a useful service in the church. Confirmation is not a sacrament. In Matthew 28:19 we have the command of Jesus to baptize, and in Luke 22:19 we have the command of Jesus to partake of the Lord's Supper.

*Visible Elements* - By visible elements we mean things which we are able to see, handle, taste or feel. In baptism, water is the visible element. In the Lord's Supper, it is the bread and the cup containing the fruit of the vine.

*God's Grace* - Through the sacraments, God comes to us individually and offers us His grace, His free gift of

forgiveness, eternal life and salvation. Through the sacraments, God's Word comes to us in a personal and individual manner.

## What Is Baptism?

The *Explanation of Luther's Small Catechism* says,
"Baptism is not merely water but it is water used according to God's command and connected with God's Word."
Some people think of baptism as just a little water being
applied to a person's head. This is not true. It is water
being applied, but it is much more. It is a means through
which God has chosen to bring His free gift to us as
individuals. Baptism is not something which we do for
God. Instead, it is God who does something for us in
baptism.

Baptism is commanded by Jesus Christ in Matthew
28:19-20. Baptism uses the visible element of water.
Baptism gives and bestows the gift of God's grace to us.
Therefore, baptism is a sacrament. It is not just a symbol
or sign of what God has done.

## The Benefits of Baptism

We have stated that God's free gift includes forgiveness of sins, eternal life and salvation. We believe that
through baptism, God offers us His free gift. Baptism is
a means of grace through which God delivers His offer to
us in a personal way. The *Explanation of Luther's Small
Catechism* says that through baptism: my sin was for-

given; I was born again; God adopted me into His family, the church; God established His covenant with me; and God gave me a way to live. Let us consider some of the passages of Scripture which deal with baptism and support this view.

*Matthew 28:19-20* - "Therefore go and make disciples of all nations, baptizing them in the name of the Father and of the Son and of the Holy Spirit, and teaching them..." We are commissioned to "make disciples." What is a disciple? A disciple is simply a follower of Jesus, that is, a Christian. In other words we are to go and make Christians. How are we to do this? Jesus said by baptizing and teaching.

Jesus said that disciples were to be made by baptizing. This is a powerful statement by Jesus. Baptism certainly is not all that there is to disciple-making. The baptized must also be taught. However, life begins not with the spreading of the truth, but with an act; and that act is an act of God. This act is baptism, and there is salvation in it. Although there is salvation in baptism, baptism is not all there is to salvation. Birth gives life, but there is more to life than birth. People must eat. What would we think of a person who insisted that an infant is neither human nor alive until he or she has eaten a hundred loaves of bread? The child must be human and alive first, and then must eat to stay alive. There are those who reason about spiritual matters in a way that would say a person becomes spiritually alive only after a certain amount of biblical knowledge has been received. Let the words of Christ stand for what they say: disciples are made by baptizing.

*Mark 16:16* - "Whoever believes and is baptized will be saved, but whoever does not believe will be condemned." Jesus places baptism on the same level with faith as a factor in salvation. Jesus must have meant what He said. If there were one hundred verses in the Bible which say that faith is necessary for salvation, and another one hundred verses which say that baptism is necessary, we would agree that both faith and baptism would be necessary for salvation. What if there were one hundred verses for baptism and only one verse for faith? Faith and baptism would still be necessary. In the Word of God only one clear verse is required to establish a doctrine. Do not be misled by some who insist that a teaching of scripture is true in direct proportion to the number of verses in the Bible that mention it.

Jesus knew that there would be some who would think that if they received baptism everything would be in order, and they would not have to worry about faith. So to make it clear, He added the word about what would happen to those who did not believe, even though they had been baptized. No such admonition is necessary to those who believe. If people truly believe, they will also seek baptism.

*John 3:5* - "Jesus answered, 'I tell you the truth, unless a man is born of water and the Spirit he cannot enter the kingdom of God.'" It has been a question whether this verse refers to baptism or not, but those who say that it does not refer to baptism are at a loss to explain what it does mean.

This verse shows us that from the beginning of His ministry Jesus had baptism in mind as a means of regeneration. In fact, there are no passages in the Bible which say there is no regeneration in baptism. Rather there are verses which support it, such as: I Peter 3:21,

Titus 3:5 and Ephesians 5:25-26. There is regeneration in baptism, but baptism is not all there is to regeneration. If there is regeneration in baptism, we can understand how disciples are made through it (Matthew 28:19-20) and why it is necessary to salvation (Mark 16:16).

*Acts 2:38* - "Peter replied, 'Repent and be baptized, every one of you, in the name of Jesus Christ so that your sins may be forgiven.'" Here repentance and baptism are placed side by side as a requirement for forgiveness. Because we are born again in baptism it is only natural that our sins should be forgiven. No one can be born again without receiving the forgiveness of sin and no one can receive the forgiveness of sin without also being born again. This verse says "be baptized...so that your sins may be forgiven." It is baptism that stands in direct relationship to forgiveness. It is a means of grace.

The Apostle Paul said, "All of you who were baptized into Christ have been clothed with Christ" (Galatians 3:27). Baptism is the means that unites us with Christ. In baptism we are covered with Christ and His righteousness which makes us acceptable before God.

## God's Gift Received

When you were an infant, you were unable to reject God's gift when it was offered to you in baptism. Today, however, it may be different as you are able to exercise your mind and will. Jesus reminds you of the free gift of God. He asks that you willingly receive it as your own.

212

# Lesson Twenty-Four     Worksheet

*True or False.*

_____ 1. The Bible says that an infant is innocent, that is, without sin.

_____ 2. When Adam and Eve sinned they brought the guilt of sin upon all people.

_____ 3. By nature we find it easier to run away from God than to flee to Him.

_____ 4. We begin to commit acts of sin when we reach the age of six.

_____ 5. The Bible tells us we have all gone astray and are going our own way.

_____ 6. We receive God's grace when we earnestly and sincerely work to obtain it.

_____ 7. Because God loves us, He will overlook our sin.

_____ 8. God has made full payment for only the sins of the believers.

_____ 9. God wants to give us the gift of forgiveness, eternal life and salvation.

_____ 10. The Bible is God's only means of offering His gift to us.

_____ 11. The Holy Spirit is the one who gives the Bible its saving power.

_____ 12. The Word of God is not needed in the sacraments.

_____ 13. All the sacred acts in the church are specifically commanded by Christ.

_____ 14. Because the sacraments are God's means of giving us His invisible grace, the visible elements are not very important.

_____ 15. We believe there are only two sacraments, baptism and confirmation.

_____ 16. Through the sacraments, God's Word comes to us in a personal and individual manner.

_____ 17. Baptism is not something we do for God, but something God does for us.

_____ 18. Baptism is just a symbol or a sign of what God has done for us.

213

_____ 19. Baptism works the forgiveness of sins and gives everlasting life to all who believe.

_____ 20. Jesus said we make disciples of all nations by baptizing and teaching.

_____ 21. We become spiritually alive only after we have received a certain amount of biblical knowledge.

_____ 22. Only one clear verse in the Bible is enough to establish a doctrine.

_____ 23. If we have been baptized, we do not have to worry about faith.

_____ 24. No one can be born again without receiving the forgiveness of sin, and no one can receive forgiveness of sin without also being born again.

_____ 25. It is impossible to reject God's free gift of grace.

*Completion Questions.*

26. Define *grace:*

27. What are the three Means of Grace?

   a.

   b.

   c.

28. What are the three requirements for a sacred act to be a sacrament?

   a.

   b.

   c.

29. Why do we say baptism is more than just a little water applied to one's head?

30. According to Acts 2:38, what is received in baptism?

*Answer the following questions from your study of Acts 24.*

31. What charges did Tertullus make against Paul?

32. How did Felix respond after Paul spoke to him about Christ?

33. Why did Felix leave Paul in prison?

# The Candidates of Baptism

## *Assignment*

Read Acts 25. Study questions 340-351 in the *Explanation of Luther's Small Catechism.* Read this lesson, complete the worksheet and be prepared for a quiz.

*When Jesus saw this, he was indignant. He said to them, "Let the little children come to me, and do not hinder them, for the kingdom of God belongs to such as these. I tell you the truth, anyone who will not receive the kingdom of God like a little child will never enter it." Mark 10:14-15*

## Is Baptism Necessary?

In Matthew 28:18-20, we have the command given by Jesus Christ, "All authority in heaven and on earth has been given to me. Therefore go and make disciples of all nations, baptizing them in the name of the Father and of the Son and of the Holy Spirit, and teaching them to obey everything I have commanded you. And surely I will be with you always, to the very end of the age." On the basis of this passage of scripture, we say that baptism is necessary because Jesus commanded it. This is reason enough.

Having discussed the value of baptism we turn now to the subject of whom to baptize. Most of the Christian churches baptize infants. This has been done from the very early days of Christianity. There are others who baptize only adults and insist that infant baptism is invalid. Scripture nowhere commands infants to be baptized nor does it command adults to be baptized. The command was to go and make disciples of all nations by baptizing and teaching them.

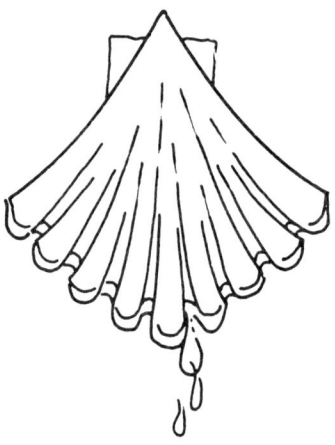

### Who Is To Be Baptized?

From the Bible passage in Matthew 28:18-20, we learn that all people are to be baptized. The only qualification is that we shall also be able to teach these people so that they may know what they have been baptized into.

In the Lutheran church, we baptize infants and children for the following reasons:

1. *Nations include children.* We believe that children are a part of the nations of which Jesus spoke. Of course, if there is no opportunity to teach them after baptism, then it will do little good to baptize. But if we have reason to believe that these infants and children will be taught the Word of God as they grow, then we have the privilege and the right to baptize them. If children are to be prevented from receiving baptism, it must be on another basis than Christ's Great Commission at the time He instituted baptism. In that command children are included fully as much as are adults. In the Lutheran church we also baptize youth and adults who may not have been baptized as little children provided they have received Jesus Christ as Savior.

2. *Children are included in the promise of God.* In Peter's sermon on the day of Pentecost he said, "Repent and be baptized, every one of you, in the name of Jesus Christ so that your sins may be forgiven" (Acts 2:38). In the next verse he said, "The promise is for you and your children and for all who are far off..." He includes children. The Greek word for *children* means *little children* and not *descendants.* Peter was sure that Christ was going to return in a short time and that there would be no time to have children. Therefore, he was not thinking of children who would yet be born, but of all people now living, children and adults.

Jesus invited the little children to come to Him and said that "to such belongs the kingdom of God." Therefore, they have the right to be received into the kingdom of God. In fact, He warns us, "Do not hinder them from coming to me."

217

3. *Children have the capacity for faith.* They do not resist the grace of God. It is as we grow older that our hearts are hardened to resist the grace of God. Although sinful by nature, the infant is receptive. What heart is more open to God than the heart of a little child where resistance is absent?

Yet we often hear the objection that an infant cannot receive the benefits of baptism because an infant cannot believe. Did not Jesus say in Mark 16:16 that faith is necessary in connection with baptism? We agree that it is. But how do you know that infants cannot believe? God's Word clearly teaches that they can. Jesus said in Matthew 18:6, "But if anyone causes one of these little ones who believe in me to sin, it would be better for him to have a large millstone hung around his neck and to be drowned in the depths of the sea."

When Jesus said to His disciples that they should permit the little children to come to Him and not hinder them, He implied that they can have faith for, "anyone who comes to him must believe that he exists" (Hebrews 11:6). In Matthew 18:3 Jesus said that if an adult will enter the Kingdom of Heaven, he must humble himself and become as a little child—that is, in simple, trusting and believing faith. It is evident from the Bible that children can believe.

Let us remember that faith is a gift of God (Ephesians 2:8) and that He creates faith in any heart that is open to Him. Certainly, the God who wants all people to be saved will not withhold the gift of faith from the needy heart of an infant who is receptive. We must remember that baptism is God's work and that the church is merely the instrument through which God gives His saving grace. Let us not put limitations on Him.

4. *Children are by nature sinners and need salvation.* The Bible clearly teaches that all are sinners, as the Apostle Paul said, "For *all* have sinned and fall short of the glory of God" (Romans 3:23). This includes infants, children, adults--everyone. "Surely I have been a sinner from birth, sinful from the time my mother conceived me" (Psalm 51:5). Children have inherited a sinful nature. There is no other nature to give them. Although they are not guilty of sinful acts, they are afflicted with sin. They are spiritually dead. They have no spiritual life. They need new life and cleansing.

Yet there are some who claim that infants are saved by innocence because they have done nothing wrong. Others say that infants are sinners, all right; but they are, nevertheless, automatically Christians. They are under the blood and involuntarily united with Christ by bonds other than faith. Still others believe that children of Christian parents, at least, are automatically children of God.

The Bible teaches that a child receives the kingdom. This fact clearly indicates that a child does not possess the kingdom, for no one receives that which he or she already possesses. Salvation means nothing to one who is not a sinner, because such a one does not need a Savior. Jesus is the Savior for sinners only. If infants are not sinners, they cannot have Jesus. Because they are sinners from birth, infants need to be saved and God offers His grace to them.

5. *Children receive God's grace only through baptism.* We believe that the only means given to us by which little children can be given God's saving grace is the Sacrament of Baptism. Jesus has commanded us to use the Sacrament for this purpose and we must obey Him. What He will do in the case of children who are not

baptized is another matter. We leave this question in His hands. God has bound us, but He has not bound Himself. He may have other ways of reaching the unbaptized with His saving grace. However, in the salvation of precious souls, the Bible teaches that God works through the preaching of the Word and the administration of the sacraments. The Bible gives no other way.

6. *Circumcision was a type of baptism.* Circumcision was the sign given to Israel at the time of Abraham as a seal of membership in His family. It was done to all male children on the eighth day after birth. It was not restrictive because any one could become a member of God's family by being circumcised. Yet no uncircumcised person, Jew or Gentile, could be counted among God's people without this sign. God did not withhold from infants the blessings of the Old Covenant but provided for their entrance into it through the rite of circumcision. Likewise, God does not withhold the blessings of the New Covenant from little children, but has provided for their entrance into it through the Sacrament of Baptism. Since God included infants in His Old Testament family there is no reason why He should withhold infants from His family today. Because circumcision was a type of baptism, we can conclude that Christian parents of the early church had their children baptized. Therefore, we continue to baptize our children.

7. *Children are a part of a household.* There is no definite record of infant baptism in the New Testament but there are records of whole households being baptized. The New Testament speaks of five households or families that were baptized. It seems possible that these included children. Therefore, we conclude that children were also baptized.

8. *Children were baptized during the time of the early church.* Many of the early church fathers such as Origen, Cyprianus and Augustine testified that infant baptism was practiced at that time. Their writings, dating from the first centuries of the church, prove that this was the universal practice for fifteen hundred years. Yet there are those who maintain that infant baptism crept into the early church in much the same way as any other heresy did. However, there was no voice that was ever raised against it on the grounds of heresy. The postponement of baptism until later in life was urged for a practical reason. It was thought that baptism washed away all sin committed before baptism but none afterwards. Therefore, it would be wise to postpone baptism until such a time in life that most sinning would be past, preferably the moment before death. So, it was not the introduction of infant baptism that was based upon a heresy but the agitation to discontinue it.

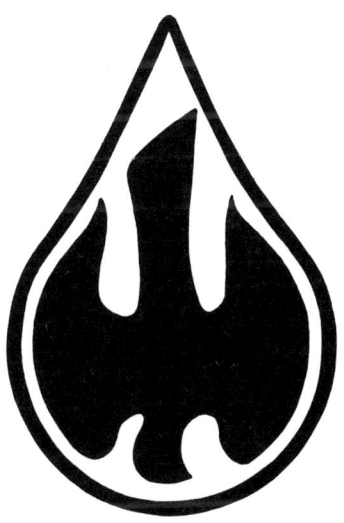

# How Are We To Baptize?

Jesus commanded His disciples to make disciples by baptizing and teaching. However, He did not tell them how to baptize. One of the basic meanings for the word *baptize* is *to wash* or *apply water*. We are to baptize by applying water "in the name of the Father and of the Son and of the Holy Spirit."

How much water are we to use? The Bible does not tell us. Some Christians think that we should use one method and other Christians think that we should use another method. The two main methods of baptizing are: immersion and pouring, sometimes also called sprinkling. Which is correct?

*Immersion* - This method is used largely by the Baptist and Pentecostal denominations. Baptism by immersion may be performed at a public worship service in the church or in a lake or river. When using this method, the person being baptized is placed entirely under the water and brought up again. In some churches the person being baptized is placed under the water three times, once each for the name of the Father, the Son, and the Holy Spirit. Churches which use this method usually do not baptize infants. They wait with the baptism until a person reaches what is called the *age of accountability*. The exception to this is the Eastern Orthodox Church, which baptizes infants by immersion.

*Pouring* - Pouring, or sprinkling, is used by Lutherans, Roman Catholics, Presbyterians, Episcopalians and Methodists. Baptism by pouring is usually performed at a public worship service of the congregation. When using this method of baptizing, the pastor usually takes a little water in his hand and pours it on the head of the person being baptized. In the Lutheran church, most people are baptized as infants. The same method is also used with people who have not been baptized in infancy.

Baptist churches insist that the only correct way to baptize is by immersion. If people have been baptized in a Lutheran church in infancy and then later in life wish to join a Baptist church, they must be baptized again by immersion. Lutherans do not require that people be baptized again if they have been baptized in a church of another Christian denomination.

We shall never be able to prove from the Bible how much or how little water is required in baptism. Since *to baptize* means *to wash* or *apply water,* we conclude that it does not make any difference how much or how little water is used.

*The Right Way* - We as Lutherans say that any method of baptism is correct as long as the water is applied in "the name of the Father, the Son, and the Holy Spirit." We say that either immersion or pouring may be used. The Bible does not tell us how much water to use, nor does it tell us how to apply the water. If this were important, Jesus would have told us which method to use and how to apply the water.

*Who Is To Baptize?* - Ordinarily, it is the pastor of the congregation who is to perform the sacred act of baptism. The church *calls* a pastor to come and preach the Word of God and administer the sacraments of baptism and the Lord's supper. However, in case of an emergency where an unbaptized person is in danger of dying before a pastor can be reached, then anyone may perform a baptism. Such a baptism is valid; and if the person lives, he or she is not to be baptized again. It should, however, be reported to the pastor of the congregation.

# Lesson Twenty-Five     Worksheet

*True or False.*

_____ 1. Jesus said we are to make disciples by baptizing and teaching them.

_____ 2. The Bible does not tell us that baptism is necessary.

_____ 3. Most Christian churches baptize infants.

_____ 4. Scripture nowhere commands infants to be baptized, neither does it command adults to be baptized.

_____ 5. The Bible does not tell us that everyone needs to be baptized.

6. Children are included, just as much as adults, in the baptism Christ instituted in the Great Commission.

_____ 7. We baptize adults only if they have received Jesus Christ as their personal Savior, provided they were not baptized as infants.

_____ 8. The promise given on the day of Pentecost was only for the adults.

_____ 9. Jesus was too busy to have anything to do with little children.

_____ 10. Though sinful by nature, the infant is receptive to the grace of God.

_____ 11. Infants cannot receive the blessings of baptism because they cannot believe.

_____ 12. Jesus said we must have the faith of an adult to enter the Kingdom of God.

_____ 13. God is able to create faith in any heart that is open to Him.

_____ 14. The Bible clearly teaches that infants are sinners and need God's grace.

_____ 15. Jesus is the Savior of sinners only.

_____ 16. The only means by which children can receive God's grace is through baptism.

_____ 17. There was no way for little children to be included in the Old Testament family of God.

_____ 18. We do not know if the early Christians practiced infant baptism.

_____ 19. A basic meaning of the word *baptize* is *to wash* or *apply water*.

_____ 20. All Christians are agreed on the method of baptism to be used.

_____ 21. Lutheran churches practice baptism mainly by immersion.

_____ 22. Baptist churches insist that pouring is the only correct way of baptizing.

_____ 23. The Bible clearly tells us how much or how little water to use in baptism.

_____ 24. Lutherans say that any method of baptism is correct, as long as it is done in the name of the Father, the Son and the Holy Spirit.

_____ 25. Any Christian may perform a baptism.

*Completion Questions.*

26. How do we know infants can believe?

27. Why do infants need to be baptized?

28. Why was baptism postponed in the early church?

29. The two main methods of baptizing are:
   a.
   b.

30. What is baptism by pouring?

*Answer the following questions from your study of Acts 25.*

31. What defense did Paul make against the charge of the Jews from Jerusalem?

32. Why did Paul appeal to Caesar?

33. How did Festus feel about Paul's guilt or innocence?

# The Fellowship of Baptism

## *Assignment*

Read Acts 26. Study questions 352-363 in the *Explanation of Luther's Small Catechism*. Read this lesson, complete the worksheet and be prepared for a quiz.

*We were therefore buried with him through baptism into death in order that, just as Christ was raised from the dead through the glory of the Father, we too may live in a new life. Romans 6:4*

## God's Offer in Baptism

We have stated that baptism is a *means of grace*. God loves all people and wants everyone to be saved by receiving His free gift of grace. Through baptism God offers us His grace which consists of forgiveness of sins, eternal life and salvation. Baptism is not something which we do for God. It is a sacrament through which God offers us His free grace.

*Forgiveness of sins* - This is God's free gift given to me in baptism. We have learned that we were all born separated from God and with a natural desire to sin. We sin because we are sinners from birth. We do not become sinners because we sin. We commit sin because we were born sinners who desired to run away from God.

*Eternal life* - This is God's free gift given to me in baptism. Eternal life is not something which we receive after we die. Instead, it is God's free gift which He wants to give us now. Romans 6:23 says, "For the wages of sin is death, but the gift of God is eternal life in Christ Jesus our Lord."

*Salvation* - This is God's free gift given to me in baptism. When we were born into this world, we were by nature sinful. But God loved us, and Christ died for us, in order that He might adopt us as His own children. To be saved means to become a child of God, to be saved from spending an eternity in hell and to live eternally in heaven with Jesus Christ.

How are we saved? How do we become children of God? John 1:12 says, "Yet to all who received him, to those who believed in his name, he gave the right to become children of God." On the basis of God's Word we may know that we are saved when we believe in Jesus. Jesus is God's free gift to us through His Word and the sacraments.

## What Does It Mean to Believe?

There are several other words which explain the word *believe*. When the Bible tells us to "believe in the Lord Jesus" (Acts 16:31), it means that we are to trust, to receive, to rely upon, to depend upon, to have faith in the

Lord Jesus Christ as our only Savior. When you trust in Jesus, then you will not depend upon your own attempts to be good so that you may go to heaven when you die. You will simply trust that Jesus died for all your sin and that He forgives you. To believe in Jesus is to take Him at His Word.

The Holy Spirit creates this faith in you through the Word of God. The faith you received from God in baptism as an infant is different from adult faith only in degree. It is not mature faith, but it is the beginning, just as the mature adult is found in the child. This infant faith must become conscious faith if it is to grow and remain spiritually alive. Therefore, it is important to know what is meant by a conscious saving faith. This faith is when a repentant and believing sinner receives Jesus Christ as Savior from sin, death, and the power of the devil, and confidently relies only upon Him. Such faith may be viewed from these three aspects:

1. *Saving faith is knowing some truths about Jesus (Knowledge).* The Gospel gives you the knowledge that Jesus is the only One whom God has sent to save you from your sin. This knowledge is not just an intellectual understanding of the facts of the Gospel, but the inner spiritual knowledge and understanding of your sin and God's grace in Christ. This is what God is seeking to give you as you read and hear His Word.

2. *Saving faith is believing that what the Bible says about Jesus is true (Assent).* If you do not give assent to, or believe, what the Bible has to say about Jesus, you do not have saving faith. Assent is not just an intellectual agreement to the truth of the Gospel, but the conviction of the heart that the Gospel has real significance for your own soul. It is to believe that you are a sinner and that Jesus died for your sins and rose again for your salvation.

3. *Saving faith is personally trusting that Jesus died for your sins (Confidence).* You are truly trusting Jesus when you receive Him as your Savior. Confidence, or trust, is the act of the will by which you completely rely upon Christ as your personal Savior. It is an act of complete surrender to Christ to have Him save you from sin. It is the very essence, the essential part, of saving faith. Without confidence you merely have belief, and not saving faith. When you trust Jesus to have mercy upon you and to save you from your sin, then you may know for sure that you have forgiveness of sin, eternal life and salvation.

## The Meaning of Baptism for Today

After baptism, then what? Does baptism have any meaning for us after it has been performed? If you have personally received God's free gift, then what? How will this affect your life?

*The free gift must be received.* In baptism God offered you forgiveness, eternal life and salvation. This is His free gift. Although you received God's forgiving grace in baptism, you need to daily continue receiving it. Admit that you are by nature a sinner and that you commit many acts of sin. You daily need God's free gift of forgiveness. God offers you His grace that you should daily accept His gift and live for Him. His promise of forgiveness and eternal life is your assurance.

*The life offered in the gift is to be lived.* When you personally receive the free gift of God, then you possess forgiveness of sins, eternal life and salvation. At the same time, the free gift places a responsibility upon you. You are now to live out this new life which has become yours. Your personal life is not to be like that of those who are lost and do not know Jesus as their Savior. Your life should really be like Jesus living His life through your body. This is to experience the full meaning and purpose of your baptism into Jesus Christ.

## The Old Life and the New Life

The old life refers to the natural desires to sin and run away from God. This is the life you have possessed since your conception and birth. If you choose to follow the desires of this old life without ever repenting, you will eventually enter into hell as a lost individual. Through the Word of God and through the Sacrament of Baptism, God has given a new life to you. It is a life in Jesus Christ. By His word of promise you may know that you shall live in eternity together with Jesus in the place He has prepared for His children.

*The Old Life* - The devil will continue to tempt you to follow after the ways of the old life. It is his desire that you should obey him in the temptations he sets before you. We call this "our sinful self, with all its evil desires."

*The New Life* - Jesus, through the Word of God and baptism, calls you to live in the new life He has given to you. You can accept this new life or reject it. If you continue to reject it, you will be lost for all eternity. If you believe in Jesus, then you know you will be saved for all eternity. This life is to be lived here and now upon this earth. It is a life which will also be continued in heaven together with Jesus.

## To Be Saved Is to Possess the New Life

What does it mean to be saved? It means to possess the new and eternal life which God has offered to me. This new and eternal life is His free gift. To be saved means that this free gift has now become mine through personal faith and belief in Jesus Christ. To be saved means to be a child of God. Are you saved? Do you possess the eternal life which God has offered to you?

## Is It Possible To Know For Sure That You Are Saved?

Is it possible to know for sure that you will go to heaven when you die? The answer is *Yes*! The Bible tells us that we may know for sure that we are saved, that we are children of God right now. The following are just a few Bible verses which speak of this assurance: I John 5:13, I John 3:2, John 5:24, Romans 8:16.

When we believe the offer of God's free gift of salvation, then we can be sure that we are children of God. God's Spirit Himself will bear witness with our spirits, telling and assuring us that we are saved, that we are His children. We should never be satisfied about our relationship to God until we know for sure that we are saved. It was natural for us not to know about this matter when we were infants. However, what was natural for us as infants is not to be natural for us today. It is natural for us to know who our physical parents are, and it should be just as natural for us to know whether or not God is our Heavenly Father. It is not a normal Christian experience to go through life without knowing whether you are saved.

## How May I Know For Sure That I Am Saved?

God wants you to know for sure that you are saved. He wants all of His children to have this assurance in their hearts. How may you be sure?

232

1. *Admit to God that you are by nature a sinner.* Acknowledge that what God says about you is true, that you are a sinner and do sinful acts. Acknowledge that you deserve the judgment of God (Psalm 51:3-5; Psalm 32:5; Romans 3:10-23; Romans 6:23).

2. *Be willing to turn from your sins.* Name them in prayer as God brings them to your mind. Do not defend any of them. Be honest with yourself and with God. If there are sinful habits of which God reminds you, be willing to give them up (Isaiah 55:7, Romans 6:12-14; I John 1:9-10).

3. *Believe the promises of God in the Bible.* Jesus Christ is the only answer. He died on the cross to pay the penalty for your sin and rose from the grave to give you new life. Trust His Word, believing that He will do what He has promised (John 3:16; Romans 5:8; II Corinthians 5:21; Romans 5:1; Romans 8:1; Acts 16:31; Ephesians 2:8-9).

4. *Invite Jesus to come into your life and save you from your sin.* Receive Him as your Savior from the guilt of sin. Give Him your life, trusting in His grace to enable you to live for Him and serve Him (Revelation 3:20; John 1:12; I John 5:11-13).

5. *Confess Jesus as your Savior to someone else.* Sharing your faith with others is the outflow of your new life in Christ. Do not be ashamed of Him. Witness to others that you have accepted Jesus as your Savior (Romans 10:9-10).

## Saved or Lost?

All people living upon the earth are either saved or lost. They are either children of God, or they are children of the devil. The Bible teaches that all people will finally spend the rest of eternity in either heaven or hell. There will be no temporary in-between place such as *purgatory* or *limbo*. The final destiny of all people one day will either be heaven or hell.

## Where Will You Spend Eternity?

God offers the possibility of heaven to you as a free gift. It is up to you to receive or reject this gift. God does not force His salvation upon anyone. He only offers it out of love for you. You may be lost in hell for all eternity by simply neglecting to receive the gift which He holds out to you. To believe in Jesus Christ is to personally take Him at His Word and accept Him and His forgiveness for all of your sins.

Where will you spend eternity? The answer is up to you. God loves you, but He hates your sin. He is willing to forgive your sin and accept you as His child if you will be willing to daily repent of your sin and receive Jesus Christ as your personal Savior. The apostle John wrote, "to all who receive him, to those who believed in his name, he gave the right to become children of God" (John 1:12).

Name _____

# Lesson Twenty-Six    Worksheet

*True or False.*

_____ 1. God wants everyone to receive His free gift of grace.

_____ 2. Baptism is something we do for God in order to receive His grace.

_____ 3. We are born with a natural desire to serve the Lord and live for Him.

_____ 4. We become sinners when we commit outward acts of sin.

_____ 5. Eternal life is not something which we receive only after we die.

_____ 6. The Bible tells us that the wages of sin is life, but that the gift of God is eternal death through Jesus Christ our Lord.

_____ 7. To be saved means to become a child of God, to be saved from spending an eternity in hell, and to live eternally in heaven with Jesus Christ.

_____ 8. We cannot know for sure in this life whether or not we are saved.

_____ 9. To believe in Jesus is to take Him at His Word.

_____ 10. We cannot be saved if we do not believe what the Bible says about Jesus.

_____ 11. We can know for sure that we have forgiveness, eternal life and salvation.

_____ 12. Baptism has no meaning for us after we have been baptized.

_____ 13. We are daily in need of God's free gift of forgiveness.

_____ 14. Your baptism into Jesus Christ does not involve your personal life.

_____ 15. The true Christian will not be tempted to follow the ways of the old life.

_____ 16. If you reject God's grace, you will be lost for all eternity.

_____ 17. The new life is to be lived here and now upon this earth and will be continued in heaven together with Jesus.

_____ 18. The new life becomes yours through personal faith in Jesus Christ.

_____ 19. It is not possible to be sure that you will go to heaven when you die.

235

20. God's Spirit Himself tells us and assures us by His word
_____ that we are His children.

21. It should be just as natural for us to know whether God has
_____ become our heavenly Father or not, as it is to know who
our physical parents are.

22. All people now living are either children of God or children
_____ of the devil.

23. The final destiny of all people is heaven or hell.
_____

24. God decides where we will spend eternity.
_____

25. We may be lost in hell by simply neglecting to accept
_____ God's free gift.

## Completion Questions.

26. The free gift God offers to us consists of:

   a.

   b.

   c.

27. Saving faith consists of what three main parts?

   a.

   b.

   c.

28. How do you experience the full meaning and purpose of
your baptism into Christ?

29. What is the difference between the old life and the new life?

30. How may you know for sure that you are saved?

## Answer the following questions from your study of Acts 26.

31. What was the message Paul preached in obedience to his
vision from heaven?

32. What did Festus say about Paul?

33. What did King Agrippa say about his becoming a Christian?

# The Sacrament of the Lord's Supper

## Assignment

Read Acts 27. Study questions 364-371 in the *Explanation of Luther's Small Catechism*. Read this lesson, complete the worksheet and be prepared for a quiz.

*Then Jesus declared, "I am the bread of life. He who comes to me will never go hungry, and he who believes in me will never be thirsty." John 6:35*

### What Is the Lord's Supper?

The *Explanation of Luther's Small Catechism* says, "The Lord's Supper instituted by our Lord Jesus Christ, is His true body and blood in, with and under the bread and wine, given to Christians to eat and to drink.

### How Did This Sacrament Come Into Being?

From the Bible (Matthew 26:20-29; Mark 14:12-25; Luke 22:7-19; and I Corinthians 11:23-32) we learn that the Lord's Supper came into being at the time of the

Jewish Passover celebration. Each year the Jews gathered together for this celebration. It was an event in which they remembered how God had delivered their ancestors from slavery and bondage in Egypt (Read Exodus 12:1-13).

On the night before Good Friday, the day of Jesus' crucifixion upon the cross, He gathered together with His disciples to eat the Passover supper in the city of Jerusalem. After the supper meal was finished, Jesus took the elements of the supper and instituted a new supper for His disciples to celebrate. Jesus knew that He was soon to be crucified. Before this was to take place, Jesus wanted to leave His disciples with a new supper by which they might remember Him.

Just as the Passover supper was by the Jewish people eaten in remembrance of their deliverance from the slavery of Egypt, so the new supper would be eaten in remembrance of Jesus Christ, who was delivered from the bondage of sin and death. In this supper, His disciples would be reminded of the human birth of Jesus, His sinless life upon earth, His suffering and death upon the cross, His resurrection from the dead and the promise of His coming again. This supper would be in remembrance of a new passover. When we turn to the Lord in repentance and faith, He will forgive, or pass over the guilt of our sin.

## "This Is..."

What did Jesus mean when He said to His disciples as He gave to them the bread and the cup, "This is my body" and "This is my blood?"

The people who have received the Sacrament of the Lord's Supper through the centuries have not been agreed upon what Jesus meant by those words.

*The Roman Catholic Explanation* - The Roman Catholic Church calls this sacrament the Mass. In the Mass, they use the elements of the bread and the cup. At a particular time in the service of the Mass, they teach that the elements, the bread and the wine, change into the body and blood of Christ. The bread is no longer bread, and the wine is no longer wine. As this happens, the priest offers up the body and blood of Christ as a sacrifice to God for the sins of the people.

*Non-Lutheran Protestant Explanation* - Most of the non-Lutheran Protestant churches hold to a symbolic explanation of the sacrament. They use the same elements in the celebration of the Lord's Supper. In their explanation of what Jesus meant by His words they take a position opposite to that of the Roman Catholic Church. They say Jesus meant that the elements, the bread and the wine, represent or symbolize His body and blood.

*The Lutheran Explanation* - Lutherans teach that the elements which are used in the sacrament do not go through a change such as the Roman Catholic Church believes. The elements always remain the same.

However, Lutherans do believe that *in, with* and *under* these elements, the *body and blood* of Jesus Christ is received. In other words, Lutherans believe that Jesus Christ is truly present in the sacrament and that He gives of Himself to each person who eats and drinks of the elements in the supper. The Lutherans teach the *Real Presence*, which means that Jesus is present in the sacrament.

The question is often asked, "How can this be?" To this we say there is no answer. It is a matter of revelation. Jesus said, "This is my body," and "This is my blood."

239

We cannot explain just how this takes place. We simply believe it. The most important thing is not that we understand everything about the supper, but that we believe Jesus Christ is truly present. In the sacrament of the Lord's Supper we meet Jesus Christ. To us the Lord's Supper is both a memorial feast and a sacrament. It is a means of grace whereby God offers to us the forgiveness of sins.

We might picture the above explanations in the following way. In the various explanations, the parts through which the line is drawn are missing in the sacrament.

| Roman Catholic Church | Lutheran Church | Non-Lutheran Protestants |
|---|---|---|
| ~~Bread~~ | Bread | Bread |
| ~~Wine~~ | Wine | Wine |
| Body of Christ | Body of Christ | ~~Body of Christ~~ |
| Blood of Christ | Blood of Christ | ~~Blood of Christ~~ |

## The Benefits of the Lord's Supper

We believe that God's free gift of forgiveness, life and salvation is offered to the believing sinner in this sacrament. The more we grow in the Christian life and experience, the more we will sense our deepest need of God's forgiveness, life and salvation. We possess this free gift of God when we trust in Jesus Christ as Savior. The longer that we are a Christian, the more we will feel our continuing need of this free gift. It is not enough to know that we have been saved once in the past. We must also have the continuing assurance that we are saved this very moment. God offers this assurance to those who trust in Jesus Christ as they eat the bread and drink the wine in the sacrament of the Lord's Supper. God wants us to know that we are Christians. Through the Lord's Supper He wants to strengthen us in this knowledge.

240

The Lord's Supper is given Christians to be a source of strength in the Christian life. The devil often comes to tempt them to doubt the Word of God about the forgiveness of sins. It is in the Lord's Supper that there is a vivid reminder that Jesus did die for all of our sins. This is one of the benefits which comes to us as Christians when we eat and drink in remembrance of Jesus Christ.

## Names Used for the Sacrament

Various names have been given to this sacrament of fellowship with Jesus Christ.

1. *Lord's Supper* - This is the name given to the sacrament in the Bible (I Corinthians 11:20). It is called the Lord's Supper because the Lord Jesus gave us this sacrament. He first prepared it and gave it to His disciples the night before He was crucified upon the cross.

2. *Holy Communion* - The sacrament is called Holy Communion because it is a sacrament of fellowship. The word *communion* means *fellowship*. There is first of all fellowship with the crucified and risen Lord Jesus Christ. Secondly, there is fellowship with other believers at the communion table. The word *communion* also expresses the union of the bread with Christ's body, and of the wine with His blood. In I Corinthians 10:16-17 we read, "The cup of blessing which we bless, is it not a communion of the blood of Christ? The bread which we break, is it not a communion of the body of Christ? For we, being many, are one bread and one body; for we all partake of that one bread" (New King James Version). The important part is that we have believed God's promise of salvation and that we belong to Him. Otherwise we will be eating and drinking at a table which does not rightly belong to us. We will be eating and drinking judgment upon ourselves.

3. *Lord's Table* - This sacrament is often called The Lord's Table because we actually eat and drink earthly elements in the sacrament. By the earthly elements we mean the bread and the wine which is used in the sacrament. We are accustomed to eating and drinking from the tables in our homes. In the sacrament, we are eating and drinking from the Lord's Table. He is the host. He is the One who prepares the table.

4. *Eucharist* - The Eucharist is a name which comes from a Greek word meaning *to give thanks*. The sacrament is sometimes called by this name because it is a supper to be received with thanksgiving. When Christians come to participate in this sacrament it should always be with the spirit of thankfulness for what the Lord Jesus Christ has done for their salvation.

5. *Sacrament of the Altar* - The Lord's Supper is also called the Sacrament of the Altar because it is celebrated at the altar. The sacrament may also be served while the people remain seated.

6. *Breaking of Bread* - The passover bread originally used was unleavened bread. It was broken so that all could eat. This is a biblical term found in Acts 2:42.

## The Lord's Supper Is For Christians

The Lord's Supper is intended only for those who are saved, those who know Jesus Christ as Savior. The children of God receive the forgiveness of sins, and are strengthened to live for Jesus Christ as they commune regularly with other believers and with the Lord Jesus Christ.

# Lesson Twenty-Seven    Worksheet

*True or False.*

_____ 1. The Lord's Supper as instituted by Christ is only for Christians.

_____ 2. The Lord's Supper came into being at the time of Pentecost.

_____ 3. God used Abraham for the deliverance of His people out of Egypt.

_____ 4. On the night of that first Passover, God passed over only the households where the blood was applied to the doorposts.

_____ 5. The first Lord's Supper was held on Good Friday.

_____ 6. After eating the Passover, Jesus instituted a new supper whereby His disciples would remember Him.

_____ 7. When we turn to the Lord in repentance and faith, He will pass over the guilt of our sin.

_____ 8. Everyone is agreed on what Jesus meant when He said, "This is my body. "

_____ 9. The Roman Catholic Church teaches that in the Mass, the elements are no longer bread and wine, but that these change into the body and blood of Christ.

_____ 10. Lutherans believe that there are four elements present in Holy Communion.

_____ 11. The non-Lutheran Protestants believe that the bread and wine are Christ's body and blood.

_____ 12. Lutherans believe that the bread and wine represent or symbolize Christ's body and blood.

_____ 13. The Bible clearly explains what takes place in the Lord's Supper.

_____ 14. In the Sacrament of the Lord's Supper, we personally meet Jesus Christ.

_____ 15. The Lord's Supper is both a memorial feast and a means of grace.

_____ 16. We do not believe there is any forgiveness offered in the Lord's Supper.

_____ 17. The longer we live as a Christian, the more we feel we need God's grace.

_____ 18. The Lord's Supper has nothing to do with the assurance of salvation.

_____ 19. The Lord's Supper was given to be a source of strength to the Christian.

_____ 20. The Lord's Supper is a vivid reminder that Jesus died for all our sins.

_____ 21. The Lord's Supper is often called *Holy Communion* because it is a sacrament of thanksgiving.

_____ 22. It is not wrong for an unbeliever to take part in the Lord's Supper.

_____ 23. The earthly elements in the Lord's Supper are the bread and the wine.

_____ 24. We should always come to the Lord's Supper in a spirit of thankfulness.

_____ 25. The Bible refers to the Lord's Supper as "The Breaking of Bread."

*Completion Questions.*

26. As a feast of remembrance, how are the Passover and the Lord's Supper alike?

27. What is the non-Lutheran Protestant view of the Lord's Supper?

28. What is meant by the *Real Presence* in the Lord's Supper?

29. How is the Lord's Supper a source of strength in the Christian life?

30. What twofold fellowship is experienced in the Lord's Supper?

*Answer the following questions from your study of Acts 27.*

31. What warning did Paul give about the voyage to Rome?

32. How did Paul comfort and encourage the passengers in the midst of the storm?

33. Why did the centurion keep the soldiers from killing the prisoners?

# The Recipients Of The Lord's Supper

## Assignment

Read Acts 28. Study questions 372-382 in the *Explanation of Luther's Small Catechism*. Read this lesson, complete the worksheet and be prepared for a quiz.

*For whenever you eat this bread and drink this cup, you proclaim the Lord's death until he comes. Therefore, whoever eats the bread or drinks the cup of the Lord in an unworthy manner will be guilty of sinning against the body and blood of the Lord. A man ought to examine himself before he eats of the bread and drinks of the cup. I Corinthians 11:26-28*

## Two Sacraments

It was stated earlier in this course that there are two sacraments which we observe in the Lutheran church. The first sacrament is baptism. This is the sacrament of initiation into the Christian faith. If you were baptized as an infant, it was the first time the Lord gave to you His free gift of salvation, forgiveness, and eternal life. At that time you were baptized into Christ. You are to be assured that Jesus Christ was willing to receive you as His own child. Now that you have come to an age where you are accountable for your choices, the Lord places before you the choice of receiving for yourself what He has offered you in baptism and in His Word.

The Bible teaches that for those who have entered into baptismal grace, there comes a time when spiritual life becomes conscious and real. This can be a time of conflict and is often known as a crisis experience. This crisis is first characterized by a realization of the sinfulness of your own heart. The Holy Spirit speaks to you about your inner motives and desires, reminding you, "You live a good life, you go to church, you read your Bible and pray; but why do you do these things? Is it because you love God or is it to get self-respect and the praise of others? Is not your own goodness a cover-up for your own selfishness?" Or, is there an independent spirit of rebellion in your life which is determined to go its own way? Is there a longing in your heart for worldly pleasures, and a mind which is filled with envy and greed? In this way the Holy Spirit convicts you of your sin and shows you your need of a Savior.

The second aspect of this crisis experience is a conscious receiving of the grace of God. You come to see that you have a sinful, depraved nature that is contrary to the law of God, and that no matter how hard you try, you are not able to be good enough. The Holy Spirit shows you that Jesus is your only hope and that He alone can save you. You learn to rely only on the grace of God for salvation.

The third part of this crisis experience is that you surrender your life to the Lord Jesus Christ. By this, you approve of your parents having you baptized as an infant. However, you need to be aware of the danger of considering yourself a Christian just because you were baptized as an infant, or because you have Christian parents, live a good life, and are faithful in church attendance. These things are good and helpful in themselves, but when you rely on these things for your salvation, they only lead you into self-righteousness. This is a sure way of losing your spiritual life. It is not enough to have a form of godliness. There must be true life in the inner person. You cannot enter into a conscious fellowship with God until sin and grace have become realities to you. May God help you to yield your life to Jesus Christ.

The second sacrament is the Lord's Supper. This sacrament is intended for all baptized people who have come to repentance and faith in the Lord Jesus Christ. Other people cannot judge who is living in this experience of repentance and faith. Therefore, the Lutheran church has made provision for a period of instruction so that people may be able to examine their own souls in the light of God's Word. Then they may know for themselves when they are prepared to participate in the Lord's Supper. However, confirmation instruction does not guarantee that all who have been confirmed are rightly prepared to take part in the Lord's Supper. Only those who acknowledge their sin and seek the forgiveness and fellowship of God are invited to the Lord's Supper.

The Sacrament of the Lord's Supper is the sacrament of fellowship in the Christian church. In this sacrament we have fellowship with all others who participate. Even more important is the fact that in the sacrament we have fellowship with the Lord Jesus Christ. We believe the Lord Jesus Christ is present in the sacrament. Therefore, the Lord's Supper is a fellowship of Jesus Christ and His true believers.

## Who Should Attend Communion?

Holy Communion is intended only for a person who has been brought to the experience of repentance toward God and to the experience of personal trust or faith in the Lord Jesus Christ. Such a person is one who has received the forgiveness of sins and who seeks to live in daily fellowship with God. Feelings of unworthiness, weakness and helplessness should not keep a repentant and believing person from the Lord's Supper. It is intended for such people. The Sacrament of the Lord's Supper, however, is not intended for those who are not Christians.

The Bible clearly teaches that there are those who should not go to the Lord's Supper (I Corinthians 11:29). Who are these unworthy communicants?

1. Those who do not believe the words, "Given and poured out for you." The unbeliever, the ungodly and impenitent, the uninstructed and the wrongly instructed should not receive Holy Communion.

2. Those who live unreconciled to someone. Those who have an unforgiving spirit and carry a grudge in their heart should not receive Holy Communion.

3. Those who cannot examine themselves, such as infants and very young children, and the unconscious should not receive Holy Communion.

4. Those who partake only from custom and habit, without knowing or thinking of the meaning of the Lord's Supper, should not receive Holy Communion.

## Who Should Receive Holy Communion?

You must always remember that a Christian is not always perfect in daily living. A person who has become a Christian still has the old nature as well as the new nature. Whenever a Christian yields to the temptation of the old nature, sin has been committed. However, as soon as there is consciousness that sin has been committed against God, there is sorrow for sin and a desire for forgiveness. The Christian who lives in this daily experience of repentance and faith is the kind of Christian who should attend the Lord's Supper often.

## How Often Is Repentance and Faith Necessary?

The crisis experience of repentance and faith becomes reality when you first come to a conscious knowledge of your sin and then experience the personal forgiveness of Jesus Christ. But no sooner do you come to this conscious faith in Christ than you find yourself faced with temptation. There may come weak moments when you yield to temptation and then you find yourself sinning against the Lord again. This does not mean that you are immediately lost and need to be saved all over again. It does mean that you need to repent of your sin as a child of God and receive His forgiveness if you are to be restored into fellowship with your heavenly Father. In this sense there must be a daily and a constant experience of repentance of sin and faith in the Lord Jesus Christ.

## What Is To Be Your Attitude Toward All Known Sin?

If the experience of true repentance and faith is real in your life, then you will be growing in hatred toward all things which you know to be sin. God will give you complete victory over every temptation if only you will trust Him for it. It is when you fail to trust Him that the victory over sin is lost.

The Lord's Supper reminds you that there is victory to be experienced in the Christian life by trusting in the shed blood of Jesus Christ. There on the cross Jesus Christ paid for the *penalty* of your sins. Now since He has been raised from the dead, He lives to give you freedom from the *power* of your sins. In the Lord's Supper there is also the reminder that some day He is coming again to deliver you from the *presence* of sin. Then you will never again be tempted to sin. The Apostle Paul said, "For whenever you eat this bread and drink this cup, you proclaim the Lord's death until he comes" (I Corinthians 11:26). From the night in which Jesus was betrayed, and until his return in glory at the last day, this proclamation, "until he comes," is to be made.

## When Are You Prepared?

If you think you are worthy because you trust in yourself and not in Christ, you are unfit. But when you realize your unworthiness and your need, and trust only in Christ for your salvation, you are invited by Jesus Himself to the Lord's Supper. He welcomes you and longs to give you the blessing He has promised.

# Lesson Twenty-Eight    Worksheet

*True or False.*

_____ 1. We observe three sacraments in the Lutheran church.

_____ 2. The Sacrament of Baptism has nothing to do with God's plan of salvation.

_____ 3. When you come to the age when you are accountable for your own actions you must accept for yourself what the Lord offered you in baptism.

_____ 4. Without this conscious acceptance of God's grace you cannot be a Christian.

_____ 5. After you are baptized, there will be no conflicts or spiritual struggles.

_____ 6. The Holy Spirit only speaks to us about the things we do and say.

_____ 7. Our own goodness is often a cover-up for our own selfishness.

_____ 8. If we try hard enough to be good, we can be assured of our salvation.

_____ 9. The Holy Spirit shows us that Jesus is our only hope; that He alone can save us.

_____ 10. You can be sure you are a Christian if your parents are Christians.

_____ 11. You cannot enter into a conscious fellowship with God until sin and grace have become realities to you.

_____ 12. The Lord's Supper is only for people who have come to a true experience of repentance and faith in the Lord Jesus Christ.

_____ 13. Confirmation is to help you examine your soul in the light of God's Word.

_____ 14. Because Jesus is present in the sacrament, the Lord's Supper is a fellowship between Him and His true believers.

_____ 15. Confirmation instruction guarantees that you are rightly prepared to take part in the Lord's Supper.

_____ 16. We are encouraged to receive Holy Communion because it is a good custom.

_____ 17. A Christian is one who is perfect in all of his daily living.

_____ 18. The Bible teaches that everyone is invited to the Lord's Supper.

_____ 19. A Christian is one who has repented of sin and trusts in Jesus Christ.

_____ 20. A person who has become a Christian still has the old nature.

_____ 21. When Christians realize they have sinned, they long to be forgiven.

_____ 22. Christians live in a constant attitude of repentance and faith.

_____ 23. The Lord's Supper has nothing to do with the victory of the Christian.

_____ 24. The Lord's Supper has nothing to do with the second coming of Christ.

_____ 25. All who know Christ as Savior are invited to the Lord's Supper.

*Completion Questions.*

26. Give three parts of the crisis experience:

    a.

    b.

    c.

27. Give three kinds of unworthy communicants:

    a.

    b.

    c.

28. Who is worthy of receiving the Lord's Supper?

29. How often is repentance and faith necessary?

30. Jesus died on the cross for the _____ of our sins, to give us freedom from the _____ of our sins, and will one day deliver us from the _____ of sin.

*Answer the following questions from your study of Acts 28.*

31. What did the islanders think when they saw that Paul was bitten by a poisonous snake?

32. Why did Paul say the people of Rome would be ever hearing but never understanding the Word of God?

33. To whom did Paul say that God's salvation has been sent, and how would they receive it?

252

# Unit III - Test

## The Sacraments

*Assignment*

Review the texts and the worksheets for lessons 24-28 in this book. Review all the memory assignments in the *Explanation of Luther's Small Catechism* questions 330-382. Know the following questions very well: 331, 338, 339, 341, 351, 355, 357, 358, 364, 368, 372, 373, 378 and 382. Review Acts 24-28.

*I will instruct you and teach you in the way you should go; I will counsel you and watch over you. Psalm 32:8*

## Some Facts To Remember

*Lesson 24*

- The Bible clearly states that we are sinners from conception and birth.
- Grace is God's undeserved love, His unmerited favor toward us through Jesus Christ.

- The three means of grace which God uses to bring the offer of His gift to us are: the Bible, the Sacrament of Baptism and the Sacrament of the Lord's Supper.
- The three requirements for a sacred act to be a sacrament are: it has been commanded or instituted by Christ; it uses visible means; and it bestows God's gift of invisible grace.
- We believe that in baptism God offers His gift of grace through which He works the forgiveness of sin, delivers from death and the devil, and gives everlasting life to all who believe (Matthew 28:19-20; Mark 16:16; Acts 2:38).

*Lesson 25*

- We believe that baptism is necessary because Jesus has commanded it.
- From Matthew 28:18-20, we learn that all people are to be baptized.
- Some reasons why we in the Lutheran Church baptize infants are:

  1. Nations include children.
  2. Children are included in God's promise.
  3. Children have the capacity for faith.
  4. Children are sinners and need salvation.
  5. Children receive grace in baptism.
  6. Circumcision was a type of baptism.
  7. Children are a part of the household.
  8. Children were baptized in the early church.

- We say any method of baptism is correct (pouring or immersion) as long as it is done in the name of the Father, the Son and the Holy Spirit.

## Lesson 26

- Three aspects of a true and saving faith in the Lord Jesus Christ are:

  1. Knowing some truths about Jesus (Knowledge).
  2. Believing that what the Bible says about Jesus is true (Assent).
  3. Personally trusting that Jesus died for our sins (Confidence).

- Even though we once received God's forgiving grace in baptism, we must now daily receive it as our own to continue in that grace as God's children.
- To be saved means that God's gift has become ours through personal faith in Jesus Christ.
- You can know for sure you are saved when you confess your sins and believe God's word of promise.

## Lesson 27

- Jesus instituted the Lord's Supper only for true Christians to eat and drink.
- We believe in the *Real Presence* that is: in, with, and under the bread and the wine, the body and blood of Jesus Christ is received in the sacrament.
- We believe that God's gift of forgiveness, life and salvation is given in the Lord's Supper.
- The Lord's Supper has been given as a source of strength in the Christian life.

- The crisis experience consists of a realization of your own sinfulness, and a conscious acceptance of God's grace.
- Confirmation instruction is intended to help you to examine your heart and life, to know your relationship to Jesus Christ, and to rightly partake of the Lord's Supper. It is designed to take seriously the Word of Christ who said that we should "make disciples ... baptizing ... teaching them to observe all I have commanded you ..." (Matthew 28:19,20).
- Christians who live in the daily experience of repentance and faith should attend the Lord's Supper often, because of their own need and Christ's command.

# Conclusion and Review

*Assignment*

Study questions 383-387 in the *Explanation of Luther's Small Catechism*. Read carefully the text of this lesson. Review the questions assigned to you by your pastor.

*But if we walk in the light, as he is in the light, we have fellowship with one another, and the blood of Jesus, his Son, purifies us from all sin. I John 1:7*

## Life

Early in life you were confronted with the question, "How should I live?" You are answering this question by your daily actions and behavior. Have you accepted and applied the guidance and direction given in God's Word? Only Jesus Christ can give meaning and purpose to life.

There is an even more basic question: "Where did I come from? Why am I here? And where am I going?" Jesus said in John 10:10, "I have come that they may have life, and have it to the full." You can experience that full life *only* when you are living in fellowship with the Lord Jesus Christ, and when you are seeking to glorify Him in all you do and say. He is calling you to daily receive the peace and joy of His forgiveness and the promise of eternal life.

## Forgiveness

"If we confess our sins, he is faithful and just and will forgive us our sins and purify us from all unrighteousness" (I John 1:9). "Faithful" means that He will do what He says. Therefore, when you honestly confess your sins and forsake them, He will forgive. Yet you may be troubled because you never become good.

You need to see that since you have the old nature, which is not good and never will become good, there is a constant struggle between the old sinful nature and the Spirit of God. (Galatians 5:17). And this struggle is serious, because according to your choice, it means life or death (Romans 8:13). The choice is, will you confess your sins and trust in Christ as your Savior, or will you not confess your sins. Just to think about confessing, and to wish for forgiveness, will not help. You are to do it.

When you have confessed, God says, "I have forgiven you." You are to believe it, even if you do not feel as if you are forgiven. When you ask your mother for forgiveness and she says, "I forgive you," are you forgiven? If you say, "I don't feel it," you will never know you are forgiven. But if you believe your mother, you will know you are forgiven, not because you feel it, but because your mother said so. Taking mother at her word assures you of forgiveness. Likewise, taking God at His Word, believing that He will do what He says, will bring relief and rest to your troubled soul. This is expressed so well in these words, "God said it, I believe it, that settles it." You will always find assurance of your forgiveness outside of yourself in the person and work of Jesus Christ.

It is not enough to know what God's Word says. You are also to act upon it. By confessing your sin and making restitution as the Word commands, you will receive rest in your troubled soul and peace in your conscience. Many people have found peace with God by acting on His promises.

## Assurance

Practically everyone who has heard the Word of God will say that they believe in Jesus. But if you ask them if they are sure that they have eternal life, that is entirely a different matter. Are you sure you have eternal life?

We must make it clear that to believe is not just to have a certain amount of knowledge of Jesus Christ. Nor is it even to admit what the Bible says is true. Romans 10:10 says, "For it is with your heart that you believe and are justified, and it is with your mouth that you confess and are saved."

How do we believe with the heart? How can we be sure that we have eternal life? It is not by examining our conversion, our faith, our spirituality, or even whether we have had certain experiences, but by building on the Word of Christ alone. The only way to assurance of faith is complete trust in the Word and promises of God. Such faith and assurance comes through the grace of God as revealed in Christ, not because we consider ourselves worthy of it, but because we realize how poor and sinful we are. Unworthiness, therefore, should not keep us from coming to Christ. The fact is that in no other way can we come to Christ than as unworthy sinners. "We pray," says Luther, "because we are unworthy to pray or to receive grace. For this reason we become worthy to pray and to receive grace. For this reason we shall also be heard and our prayers shall be granted. Since we believe that we are unworthy, and trust only to God's faithfulness, He will answer our petitions." (*A Faithful Guide to Peace with God*, by C. O. Rosenius, Augsburg Pub. House, page 236) We are to hold fast to the promises of God, for out of grace and mercy He will forgive all our sins and assure us of salvation.

Assurance is the work of the Holy Spirit. The Apostle Paul writes, "The Spirit himself testifies with our spirit that we are God's children" (Romans 8:16). It is at the cross that the Holy Spirit shows us what we have in the Savior. The final solution which opens to us all the glories of heaven is found at the cross, as our assurance of salvation is based solely on what Jesus has done for us. It is in looking to Jesus that we will be sure that our sins are forgiven, that we are loved of God and that we are His children.

The entire First Epistle of John is written "that you may know that you have eternal life" (I John 5:13). How does this epistle give us assurance of salvation? First it speaks to us regarding our attitude toward sin. We read, "If we claim to have fellowship with him yet walk in the darkness, we lie and do not live by the truth" (I John 1:6). If we try to hide our sin, or say that we have not sinned, we cannot be a child of God.

"But if we walk in the light, as he is in the light, we have fellowship with one another, and the blood of Jesus, his Son, purifies us from all sin" (I John 1:7). To walk in the light means that we have confessed our sins rather than hid them. Sin must be confessed or there can be no assurance. As the Scripture says, "He who conceals his sins does not prosper, but whoever confesses and renounces them finds mercy" (Proverbs 28:13). This is a tremendous truth. When we confess our sins, we find that God's promise is good. Can there be anything more wonderful than to know that we are cleansed by our Lord Jesus Christ?

Secondly, First John speaks to us about our attitude toward the Word of God. "We know that we have come to know him if we obey his commands" (I John 2:3). There can be no assurance which is not based upon a right relationship to the Word of God. Just as a newborn baby desires milk, so the one who has new life in Christ hungers for the Word of God. Nothing else can satisfy. Such a person has learned the truth of Jesus' words, "You are already clean because of the word I have spoken to you" (John 15:3). It is serious to neglect or reject God's Word. But the promise is given, "if anyone obeys his word, God's love is truly made complete in him" (I John 2:5). Such assurance is real. It is the work of the Holy Spirit.

Thirdly, First John says, "this is how we know that he lives in us: We know it by the Spirit he gave us" (I John 3:24). However, we are warned to "prove the spirits," because it is possible for a spirit not of God to give false assurance. When "The Spirit himself testifies with our spirit that we are God's children" (Romans 8:16), we will know it. For, "where the Spirit of the Lord is, there is freedom" (II Corinthians 3:17), and "the mind controlled by the Spirit is life and peace" (Romans 8:6). This assurance cannot be entirely described in words. However, it is an inward joy that cannot be compared to any other joy found in this world. As the Scripture says, "He who has the Son has life; he who does not have the Son of God does not have life" (I John 5:12).

Perhaps you have never received the saving grace of God in Christ. Why not do so now?

How can the Holy Spirit assure you that you have eternal life if you have never definitely invited Christ into your life? Naturally, no one can be forced to receive Christ. If you are willing, pray this prayer: "I come to you now Lord Jesus. I confess that I am a sinner and that I have sinned against you. I believe that you died for my sins. Forgive me and help me to turn away from my sin. I receive you now as my Savior. Come into my life and help me to live for you. And make my life a blessing to others. Amen."

Thank God that He has forgiven you and that He has given you eternal life. You will have struggles and the devil will tempt you, but be assured that the Word of God has the answer to all your problems. Christ is able and willing to give peace to your heart and victory over your sin. "But thanks be to God! He gives us the victory through our Lord Jesus Christ" (I Corinthians 15:57).